YOUR BLUEPRINT FOR THAT WINNING EDGE

In any current business climate, the difference between flourishing and failing is quite simply whether or not the boss has mastered the vital basics of planning and leading the enterprise. Now two of America's top business consultants tell you in plain, no-nonsense language the vital do's and don'ts of

—Calculating the market for your goods and services
—Finding and motivating good employees
—Identifying and eliminating trouble spots
—Maintaining quality
—Pleasing customers
—Checking out the health of your company

and everything else you need to do on a day-to-day basis to make sure your business thrives over the years.

THE COMPETITIVE EDGE

Fran Tarkenton has achieved the outstanding double triumph of being both a Hall of Fame football quarterback and a hugely successful entrepreneur and consultant. He is the chairman and chief executive officer of KnowledgeWare Inc., which was ranked #2 in *Business Week*'s list of Best Small Growth Companies in the United States. His books include *Playing to Win* and *How to Motivate People*. He lives in Atlanta.

Joseph H. Boyett is an internationally recognized management consultant and coauthor of *Workplace 2000*.

THE
COMPETITIVE EDGE

Essential Business Skills for Entrepreneurs

Fran Tarkenton and
Joseph H. Boyett

A PLUME BOOK

PLUME
Published by the Penguin Group
Penguin Books USA Inc.; 375 Hudson Street,
New York, New York 10014, U.S.A.
Penguin Books Ltd, 27 Wrights Lane, London W8 5TZ, England
Penguin Books Australia Ltd, Ringwood, Victoria, Australia
Penguin Books Canada Ltd, 10 Alcorn Avenue
Toronto, Ontario, Canada M4V 3B2
Penguin Books (N.Z.) Ltd, 182–190 Wairau Road,
Auckland 10, New Zealand

Penguin Books Ltd, Registered Offices: Harmondsworth, Middlesex, England

First published by Plume, an imprint of New American
Library, a division of Penguin Books USA Inc.

First Printing, October, 1991
10 9 8 7 6 5 4 3 2 1

With the exception of the Preface and Chapter 18, the contents of this book first
appeared, in different form, as a series of articles in *Entrepreneur* magazine.

 REGISTERED TRADEMARK—MARCA REGISTRADA

LIBRARY OF CONGRESS CATALOGING IN PUBLICATION DATA:
Tarkenton, Fran.
    The competitive edge : essential business skills for entrepreneurs
/ Fran Tarkenton and Joseph H. Boyett.
      p.   cm.
    ISBN 0-452-26682-3
    1. New busines enterprises—Management.   2. Entrepreneurship.
3. Success in business.   I. Boyett, Joseph H.   II. Title.
HD62.5.T36   1991
658.4'21—dc20
                                                      91–9819
                                                      CIP

Printed in the United States of America
Designed by Eve Kirch

BOOKS ARE AVAILABLE AT QUANTITY DISCOUNTS WHEN USED TO PROMOTE PROD-
UCTS OR SERVICES. FOR INFORMATION PLEASE WRITE TO PREMIUM MARKETING
DIVISION, PENGUIN BOOKS USA INC., 375 HUDSON STREET, NEW YORK, NEW YORK
10014.

Contents

Preface

You need a competitive edge whether you are already running a small business or just thinking of starting one. Why? Because without an advantage, your chances of success aren't good. The sad fact is that most new businesses fail in the first five years. The traditional estimate has been that four out of five new companies fail in the first five years. That may not be entirely true: for example, in the late 1980s Bruce Kirchoff, a professor at Babson College, and Bruce Phillips, an economist at the Small Business Administration, examined an extensive data base on new companies. They found that nearly 40 percent of new companies survived six years or longer. Regardless of whether the true statistic is four out of five or only four out of ten, small businesses still have a high mortality rate.

Given that an uncomfortably large number of start-up businesses fail, does that mean you should give up your dream of being an entrepreneur? Not necessarily. First, consider why so many small businesses fail. The fact is that most businesses go out of existence for one of two reasons: lack of capital or poor management. Of the two reasons for business failures, poor management is the most common. Obviously, it's nice to have lots of capital. But even with lots of capital to work with, if you waste all that money, your business may still fail. On the other hand, if you have a good grasp of essential management skills, you are less likely to run out of funding before your business has a chance to take off. Plus, with good management skills you'll find it much easier to convince your financial backers to extend you that small amount of additional funding to help you survive the tough times and turn what could be just another business failure into a roaring success. We can't give you the capital to start or run your business. We can offer you the essential business skills. That's what *The Competitive Edge* is all about.

In the chapters that follow, we will give you tips and techniques to help you succeed. We'll show you how to develop a business strategy, hire and train people, motivate employees, and deal with customers. We'll also show you how to manage your time, delegate to your staff, and deal effectively with problem employees and problem customers. Read and apply what we suggest in the pages that follow and we are confident you will give your business a better chance of success and, at the same time, reduce the strain and stress all entrepreneurs encounter.

The advice, tips, and techniques contained in this book grew out of the experiences of consultants in our consulting firm, Tarkenton Conn & Company. For over twenty years, they have trained managers and owners of American businesses in essential business skills. Based upon our consultants' experiences, we have chosen to cover in this book those skills that we have found to be most critical for helping executives improve performance. We have also boiled down the tools and techniques to a few short pages on each skill. You can read this book from beginning to end and cover all of these skills in a few hours. Or you can just pick out those specific chapters that cover areas of most benefit to you right now. However you read this book, we think you will find it filled with simple, practical advice you can put to work right away.

In preparing this book, we are indebted to a number of people. In particular, we would like to thank Hank Conn, President of Tarkenton Conn & Company, for his advice and willingness to devote company resources to the preparation of this book. We would also like to thank Tarkenton Conn trainers and consultants Shirl Handly, Dot Mohr, Edith Onderick, Vicki Silvers, Mark Dillard, and Michele Williams for their advice and willingness to share their considerable knowledge. In particular, we would like to thank Leigh Ann Conn for her diligent, timely, and professional assistance in preparing the manuscript of this book. Finally, we would like to thank Clare Thain, publisher, Rieva Lesonsky, editor, and the excellent staff of *Entrepreneur* magazine. It was Clare's suggestion for an original series of articles for *Entrepreneur*, published during 1988 and 1989, that led to this current book. Needless to say, the current book would not have been possible without their continuing faith and support for what we were trying to do. All of the above deserve credit for what is right about this book. Any errors, mistakes, or omissions are ours alone.

__1__

Developing Your Business Strategy

Okay, you have a dynamite idea for a business. Perhaps it is a hobby you know you can turn into a money-making success. Perhaps you have just gotten tired of someone else making money off your knowledge and skill. Regardless of how your idea for a business evolved, you will greatly increase your chances of making your business a success if you will take the time to develop not just a business plan but a real "business strategy." A well-thought-out business strategy can help you make your company unique and can guide you to make the kind of day-to-day decisions that are right and will enable your company to prosper and grow.

Why You Need a "Business Strategy"

Why do you need a formal, written "business strategy"? Simple. You need a strategy if you hope to beat your competition.

Regardless of how good your idea for a new business happens to be, chances are someone has already thought of it or, if they haven't developed an idea of their own, they'll be very happy to steal yours. In short, no matter what type of business you start, you will have competition, or at least the potential for competition. You need a plan—a business strategy—outlining how you are going to beat that competition.

Taking the time to sit down and carefully write out a business strategy is probably not something you relish doing. If you are like most entrepreneurs, you would rather just get on with starting your business. Yet there are two good reasons why you should take the time to develop a written strategy.

First, the process of developing a written business strategy will help you clarify your thinking about your business. In our experience, small business people all too often tend to make their decisions on the fly without due regard for the future implications of those decisions or how one decision can impact others. The process of putting together a written strategy will force you to think through your business. Then when you do have to make quick decisions, you will have some basic guidelines to ensure that you make the right decisions.

Second, a written business strategy is a critical management tool. To assist you in running your business, you will have to hire employees, and if they are to serve you well and not have to come to you for every decision, they need a sense of common purpose or direction and guidelines they can follow in making their own decisions. In short, they must understand your business, where it is going, and what is critical to make it a success. A written business strategy is an invaluable aid to help you communicate your "vision" to the people who work for you.

Format for a Strategic Business Plan

There are many books and articles that suggest formats for a written business plan. Most of these suggest that you include a business mission statement, discussion of product/service lines, sales projections, and more. Unfortunately, such plans too often become financial/numbers exercises. While we think that a solid analysis of the numbers and your expectations for return/profit and so on are important, in our opinion a good business strategy should go far beyond tables, charts, and numbers. Here are the major components of a business strategy that will give you not only financial and sales targets to meet, but a complete plan for running your business.

Statement of Basic Values and Fundamental Beliefs

Often overlooked in traditional business plans, this statement spells out the fundamental principles upon which your company is based. By developing and living by such a statement, you will go a long way toward making your company something that is truly special for your employees, customers, and the community itself.

Mission Statement

This should be a clear and concise statement that can serve as a guide you follow in making decisions about the products/services you will offer and the markets/customers you will serve. No business should try to provide every possible product or service to every conceivable market or customer. Every business—if it is to be successful—must focus on some segment of the marketplace where it can compete because it has special capabilities or a special advantage. Your mission statement should spell out clearly the business you are in and should be your guide to new products/services to offer and new markets/customers to serve.

Analysis of Your Competition

As we said, you always have competition or the potential for competition. In this segment, you carefully examine your competitors—who are they and what are your strengths and weaknesses when compared to them?

The Key Areas in Which You Choose to Compete

Essentially, all businesses compete in one or more of twelve basic areas including such areas as cost, quality, and customer service. We will describe each of these areas and show you how to pick the areas where your business can successfully compete. Deciding how you will compete is a critical step since by doing so you are deciding how you will take the fight to your competition. Obviously, you are looking to compete in the area(s) where you have the advantage.

Your Key Capabilities

Once you decide how you are going to compete, you will immediately see that you need to acquire and maintain certain capabilities or assets. These could be human resources, financial resources, or a particular technology, for example. Regardless, once you have determined how you will compete, you have to plan for obtaining and maintaining the assets, capabilities, and resources you need for success. You spell these out in this section of your plan.

Assessment of Return/Profit

This is the numbers/financial section of your plan which is based upon the decisions you have made in the first five sections. In working through this section, you may discover that you must go back and revise previous sections because the numbers just don't work.

Plan for Communicating and Implementing Your Strategy

This is the action-oriented section of your plan. It spells out what you and your employees will do and when you will do it. Without this section and your execution of the action steps you identify in this section, your strategy is nothing more than wishful thinking.

Developing Your Business Strategy

To develop your business strategy, you need to work through each of the sections of the plan we outlined just now. To help you, we will suggest a process to follow. But don't try to develop your plan alone. We suggest you involve not only your partner(s) or business associates, but also any key employees you have brought in to help you run the business. If you haven't started your business yet and you don't have a partner, ask some of your friends or relatives or your spouse to help you develop your strategy. Try to assemble a group of at least four or five people to work with you. Developing a business strategy is a thinking process. You'll do your best thinking if you have someone to work with—someone you can bounce ideas off and who can ask you good questions and give you good advice.

Your Basic Values and Fundamental Beliefs

If your business is to succeed in the long run, it must stand out from the crowd. There must be something about your business that sets it apart from all of the other businesses in your community or even in the world. Here, we aren't just talking about the kind of products or services you offer. We are talking about something much more than that. No matter how unique your product or service, there will always be someone else who can provide the same product or service, perhaps as cheaply and as well. Your business, if it is to stand out from the rest, must have some special difference—some flair. Deciding upon that special quality which will characterize your business is your first step toward developing a business strategy.

How do you define that special "flair" for your business? You and your team should answer the following questions.

How should we treat our customers?

Obviously, customers are the lifeblood of every business. In fact, it can be said that the sole purpose of a business—any business— is to attract and keep customers. Really successful businesses are characterized by the special relationship they establish with their customers. Many businesses have survived stiff competition and hard times largely because they had a loyal customer base that stuck with them. Thinking about that "special relationship" you want to establish with your customers, consider businesses you have worked for or conducted business with. What did you like and dislike about the way they treated their customers?

How should we treat our employees?

Next to customers, perhaps the most important asset you will have in running a business is your employees. You will have to attract and keep the best people if you hope to make your business a success. Attracting the best people won't be easy. They're in great demand. Obviously, one way to attract the best people is to offer really attractive salaries and fringe benefits. But money is rarely enough. Anyway, as a start-up business, you may not be able to afford to pay the highest rates. You'll have to offer something more than money if you want to attract the best. What is that something more? We think it's the kind of work environment you create. Today, most people want a lot more from their job than just a paycheck. Most want respect, to be listened to, to feel a part of the business, to feel as if they are accomplishing something of importance with the work they do. Think about how you can create that kind of special work environment in your business. Make a list of things you should do to create that special environment. For example, you might list such things as

- Keep communication informal
- Work as a team
- Have open exchange of ideas (even those I don't like)
- Treat people fairly

How should we treat our suppliers?

Another important group for the success of your business is your suppliers—all those companies and people who will provide the products and services your business will require to serve its customers. Just as you can't run a successful business without good relations with your customers and employees, you can't be a success without a good relationship with your suppliers. Every business occasionally must call on its suppliers for some special favors—to extend a little more credit, to make a priority delivery, to provide a special service. If you have built a strong, positive, working relationship with your suppliers, they will be much more likely to respond to your special needs. Ask yourself how you should treat your suppliers to ensure that you build that relationship.

What is our responsibility to the community?

Obviously, you are in business to make money. But making money shouldn't be your sole objective. You should also be in business to provide a service to people in your community. Your efforts to help your community are not just good public relations or something nice to do. In the long term, the economic, environmental, and social welfare of the community where your business is located will have much to do with the success of your business. After all, both your employees and customers are likely to be drawn from that community. If the community as a whole thrives, your business can't help but benefit. As a small, start-up business, your ability to help the community may be limited. But think of the kinds of things you can do to help the community right from the start, such as setting up bins to recycle paper and other recyclable waste materials created in your business operations.

What are our responsibilities to our investors and other financial partners?

Chances are you obtained financial support from others to enable you to start your business. Now is the time to be specific about your responsibilities to people and institutions that provided your business with financial backing. Obviously, you have a responsibility to provide them with a reasonable return on their investment, repay loans, provide financial reporting, and so on. But you should also be concerned about the relationship you build with these people. As your business grows, you will need additional funding for such things as expansion, modernization, and the purchase of new technology. You will greatly enhance your ability to obtain this additional funding if you have built a strong and positive relationship with those who put their trust in you in the past.

What should our relationship be with other major stakeholders?

In addition to customers, employees, suppliers, your community, and investors, you may have other major stakeholders—people or institutions that have an interest in and influence on the success of your business. For example, your business may be governed by federal, state, and/or local regulators. Or your relationship with and/or participation in professional associations may be critical to the success of your business. Discuss the kind of relationship you want to establish with these other "stakeholders" and how you will create that relationship.

When you have completed answering these questions, you should have a fairly complete inventory of your responsibilities, obligations, and the dos and don'ts of how you want to run your business. You should write up a statement outlining what you have discovered. This document spells out what you believe in and what makes your company special. It's a document you should share with your employees and one you should refer to frequently to guide you in your day-to-day decisions.

With your value statement in hand, you have finished the first section of your strategic plan. Next, you need to decide upon a "mission" for your business.

Your Mission Statement

Developing your mission statement should be easy—right? After all, a mission statement is nothing more than just a few sentences describing your business. You already know the kind of business you want to run—a restaurant, a compact disc store, a print/copy shop, etc. What more is there to developing a mission statement than just writing down a few words or sentences stating what you plan to do? A lot more.

If a mission statement is to be of any help to you, it must go beyond a mere descriptive statement. A good mission statement clearly defines your business in terms of both the products/services you intend to offer and the markets/customers you intend to serve. You must carve out a specific niche—a specific business segment in which you intend to compete in order for your business to be a success in the long term. Another secret for long-term success is to ensure that as your business grows, you don't get too far afield from your basic "core" expertise. In short, today in business you have to be very good to survive. You can't be good in everything, so you must focus. A well-thought-out mission statement will give you that focus by answering two fundamental questions about your business: What type of products/services will you provide? What type of markets/customers will you serve? Before you can write your mission statement, you have to answer these two questions. How do you answer them? By identifying what is called your driving force.

The concept of a "driving force" for a business was first suggested by Benjamin B. Tregoe and John W. Zimmerman in their book, *Top Management Strategy*. The idea of a driving force is expanded upon in *Maximum Performance Management*, by Joseph H. Boyett and Henry P. Conn. Here, because of space limitations, we can only discuss the driving force concept briefly, so we suggest you check either of these two books for more information.

Tregoe and Zimmerman define the driving force for a business as "the primary determiner of the scope of future products and markets." Once you select a driving force for your business—and there can be only one driving force—you have established the focus for your business. You select all of the future products/services you offer and markets/customers to be consistent with the driving force you have selected.

In their book, Tregoe and Zimmerman discussed nine possible driving forces. In *Maximum Performance Management*, seven of these are described in detail. Here, to give you an idea of how the driving force concept works, we will discuss the three that are most common. If none of these three are appropriate for your business, you can refer to the books we have mentioned for other suggestions.

The three driving forces we have found to be most common for American businesses are:

1. Body of knowledge
2. Product/service offered
3. Markets/customers served

If you select "body of knowledge" as the driving force for your business, you are saying that what your business offers to the public is knowledge in a specific subject area. You might offer your customers a wide variety of products or services, but they would all have one thing in common. They are all derived from the body of knowledge you possess. Likewise, you might direct your marketing and sales efforts toward a wide variety of customers. Yet they would all have one thing in common. Each would have a need for the body of knowledge you possess and can provide to meet their needs. In short, your body of knowledge dictates both the products/services you offer and the markets/customers you serve. If a product or type of service doesn't require or isn't derived from your particular body of knowledge, then it isn't right for your company. If a market or customer doesn't have a need that can be satisfied through the application of your body of knowledge, then that customer isn't right for your business and you wouldn't waste your marketing and sales effort on him or her.

If you select "product/service offered" as your driving force, then you are taking a slightly different approach to defining your business. In this case, what you are bringing to the public is the ability (knowledge/skill, production capability, servicing capability, etc.) to produce a specific type of product or provide a specific type of service. Once you select your initial product or service offering, then all future products or services you offer will be very similar to those you already offer. In respect to the type of customers you serve, they may be quite different (in terms of age, sex, income, etc.), but they will all have one thing in common— a need for the particular type of product/service you offer.

The third, and final, possible driving force we will discuss here is "markets/customers served." Here, the focus of your business is meeting the needs of a particular type of customer (old people, young people, women, men, the rich, the poor, etc.). The kinds of products/services you will offer can vary greatly. The only thing they have in common is that they are something needed by your target customer.

As you read the preceding material, you may have said to yourself, "All of these apply to me." In fact, you may be right. There are usually a number of different ways you could define your business, just as there are thousands of possible businesses. The beauty of the driving force is that it forces you to define your business in just one way. It makes you focus on doing one thing well, which is exactly what you want to do.

To illustrate just how important the selection of your driving force or primary focus is, we will use the example of our own consulting business. At Tarkenton Conn & Company, we decided long ago that we had a body-of-knowledge driving force. In this case, our body of knowledge was our expertise in implementing innovative management and compensation practices. Everything we do stems from that body of knowledge. We train, consult, lecture, write, and engage in a variety of activities. What they all have in common is that they involve the use of the knowledge we possess. Also, we don't restrict ourselves to a particular type of customer. We work with large businesses and small businesses, in manufacturing and service, with public and private organizations. The only thing our various customers have in common is that they have a need for the knowledge we possess. Since we are in the "knowledge business," we expend a lot of effort to stay current in our particular area of expertise.

While we define ourselves as being in the knowledge business, we didn't have to do so. For example, we could have adopted a product/service focus. In this case, we might have decided that we wanted to be a training company. In fact, some of our competitors do define themselves as trainers. If we had adopted a training focus, our efforts would have been directed toward developing and offering training programs on a wide variety of subjects to meet the needs of those who purchase training.

A different focus for our firm might have been on a specific market or customer base. For example, we could have positioned ourselves as consultants to a particular type of industry or business (manufacturing or service, or even more specifically defined such as textiles, utilities, banking). Again, some of our competitors do this.

As you can see, in defining our business we had a number of choices. So do you. And you can never know for certain whether you are making the right choice. That can only be determined after the fact. If your business succeeds, then you either were lucky or, in fact, you did make the right choice. If it fails, then . . . well, we won't talk about failing. Nevertheless, how do you select among various possible driving forces? You certainly don't want to just flip a coin. Here are some suggestions.

Your first task in selecting a driving force is to narrow down your options. If you were examining all of the nine that Tregoe and Zimmerman present in their book or the seven presented in *Maximum Performance Management,* it is likely that you would immediately discard some as not applying to your business. Even with the three we have mentioned, you may have already discarded one. Regardless, as a first cut, try to get down to no more than two or three possibilities. Then weigh the pros and cons of each. Take one possible driving force at a time and ask yourself:

1. If we define our business this way, how many competitors will we have? (You want as few as possible.)
2. With this focus, how broad would our potential customer base be? (You want as large a base of potential customers as possible.)
3. How vulnerable would we be to sudden changes in economic, social, or political conditions? (You want to minimize the impact of forces out of your control.)
4. To what extent does this focus build upon knowledge, skill, production capability, research and development, and/or marketing/sales capability that we already have or can easily acquire? (All of these represent potential costs of doing business, and you want to minimize such costs.)
5. Will this focus require substantial new funding or significantly increase our debt structure?

Once you have assessed the pros and cons of several possible driving forces, one should stand out as the clear choice. With the knowledge of your driving force, the actual wording of your mission statement should be a fairly simple task. You just rewrite your driving force in the form of a mission statement. For example, if you choose body of knowledge as your driving force, you might write: "The mission of XYZ Company is to acquire and utilize knowledge in the area of . . . to meet the needs of customers who want to . . ." The exact wording of your mission statement doesn't matter. What does matter is that, in the future, anyone reading your mission statement would have little doubt concerning the types of products/services your business intends to offer and the markets/customers you intend to serve. The real test for the adequacy of your statement is whether when presented with an idea for a new product or service or a new market to enter you could go to your mission statement and, reading it, know whether that new product or market fits with your business. After all, the real test of your mission statement is not how it is worded, but whether it will serve as a useful guide in helping you make these future decisions.

Analyzing Your Competition

Regardless of the type of business you run, you always have competition or the potential for competition. There is just no doubt about that. Okay, maybe you have been lucky so far. You developed a totally new idea for a product or service. Since you were first, there was no competition. Maybe you picked a super location. There is no competition for miles around. Why should you worry? You shouldn't—unless, of course, you really did have a good idea or really did pick a good location. But if your idea was good or your location was prime, watch out. There's someone out there watching you. You may wake up one morning to find a competitor opening up right next door or just across the street. Or you may find someone peddling a product or service just different enough from yours so that your patent or copyright offers you no protection. The time to start worrying about competition is now, not after you have already started losing customers to a new upstart. Once you begin losing customers, it may be hard to get them back. You need to do some analysis now, before your competition can even get started.

Okay, so you need to analyze your competition (or potential competition). Where do you start? You make a list of your current or potential competitors. Right? Wrong. Never start analyzing your competition by first drawing up a list of your competitors. The place to start is with your customers. More specifically, the place to start is with your "ideal" customer. Why? Because you can't identify your true competition unless you thoroughly understand what your customer really buys when he or she does business with you. Sound strange? Not really.

Peter Drucker, the famous business writer, wrote in his book *Management,* "A business is not defined by the company's name, statutes, or articles of incorporation. It is defined by the want the customer satisfies when he buys a product or service." Drucker was right. To really understand your business—what it is, what it should be, and perhaps more importantly, how you can beat your competition—you must understand your customer.

To begin your competitive analysis, start by visualizing your "ideal" customer. What does he or she look like? How old is he? Where does he work? Is he rich or poor? What problems, stresses, concerns does he have? Most important, when he comes in to do business with you, what needs does he have? What kinds of problems does he look for you to resolve? Think about your interaction with your "ideal" customer in two respects—the process and the outcome. *Process* refers to the nature of the interaction—what happens in the course of the customer doing business with you. *Outcome* refers to the end product of that interaction—what he takes away when the interaction is completed. For example, in a restaurant, *outcome* refers to the quality and type of food the customer was served. *Process* refers to how the customer was treated and how the food order was handled. To understand your customer, you must understand his expectations for both process and outcome, since meeting or exceeding both of these expectations is key to your success. When considering your customer's expectations, think about what he or she might want in respect to the following:

1. *Capacity*—The volume or range of products/services offered.
2. *Rate*—Efficiency, performance, or capacity to offer products/services per hour, day, week, or other time period.
3. *Accuracy/Fitness for Use*—Perceived quality of products/ser-

vices you offer as compared to some absolute model or standard the customer has in mind.

4. *Comparative Quality*—When the customer has no absolute model or standard to refer to, the perceived quality of the product or service versus a previous or competing product or service.

5. *Uniqueness/Novelty*—The perceived quality of what you offer due to some unique or novel characteristic not available elsewhere.

6. *Timeliness*—Your ability to provide the product/service by a promised, scheduled, or target date.

7. *Throughput Time*—The elapsed time for delivery of products/services upon demand/request.

8. *Availability*—Your ability to have the product/service available on demand and as needed.

9. *Planned Cost*—Your ability to provide the product/service within an estimated or planned cost.

10. *Relative Cost*—Your ability to provide the product/service at a cost less than that of a comparable product/service.

11. *Benefit/Value*—Your ability to provide a product/service with high perceived value irrespective of relative cost.

12. *Customer Service*—The customer's perception of the care, attention, responsiveness, friendliness, concern, and so on with which you provide the products or services.

Once you have a thorough understanding of your customer and his needs and wants, then—and only then—are you ready to make a list of competitors or possible competitors. In drawing up your list, think of those businesses that could meet your customers' needs. Who are they? Where are they? Obviously, you should list businesses like yours that are close to you—down the street, around the block. But also consider businesses across town that might relocate near you. Once you have these obvious competitors listed, you should go further. Ask yourself who is not in your business now, but might get into your business because they are already in a related field? For example, if you run a restaurant, you might not initially view a grocery store as a direct competitor. But couldn't it become one? Many grocery stores have opened in-store restaurants or food take-out centers. Try to draw up as complete a list of current or potential competitors as you can.

Now that you have your list of competitors and potential competitors, you need to do some analysis. Take a sheet of paper and list your "ideal" customer's desires for both process and outcome (including the twelve areas we mentioned) down the left-hand side of the page. Across the top of the page, make two columns. Label one "Strengths" and the other "Weaknesses." Using a separate page for each competitor or potential competitor you have identified, make a list of your strengths and weaknesses versus that competitor. You can just place a check mark in each column to indicate that an area is a strength or weakness, or you can write in a clarifying comment.

Once you have completed your analysis of each competitor, you should then consolidate the results. To do your consolidation, take a new sheet and tabulate the number of times a customer's desire was a strength or weakness. For example, you might have identified twenty competitors. When you do your consolidation, you find your relative quality is a strength versus twelve competitors and a weakness versus the remaining eight.

The Key Areas in Which You Choose to Compete

In completing your competitive analysis, you developed a picture of your competition and your strengths and weaknesses versus what they could offer. Now you have to make some tough choices. Previously, we listed twelve areas of wants or needs customers have. These are also the areas in which most companies compete. But no company can compete in all twelve areas. You will be forced to narrow your areas of competition to no more than five or six. But how do you narrow your selection?

The best place to start picking the key areas in which you choose to compete is with your strengths. Look closely at what you do well versus your competition. In developing your strategy, what you want to do is to build upon your strengths, since they represent your advantages. For example, you may find that one of your strengths is benefit/value—your costs are high relative to your competition, but you deliver a lot of value for the money and, most important, your "ideal" customer prefers value over low cost.

Benefit/value then becomes an area in which you will compete and directs you to plan to maintain or enhance the "added value" of the products/services you offer. By picking your strengths first, you will find it easier to identify other areas in which you should compete. For example, if benefit/value is one of your strengths, then uniqueness/novelty may be another key area in which you will choose to compete. Why? Because you probably need to offer something unique or novel to command a higher price. In fact, if your customers prefer benefit/value to low costs, they probably also seek products or services that are—to them—unique and novel.

Your Key Capabilities

Once you have decided upon the key areas in which you choose to compete, your next step is to identify the key capabilities your business must have. Key capabilities include such things as

- A particular technology
- A body of knowledge or skill
- A production capacity or capability
- A marketing capability
- Distribution channels
- Raw materials
- Financial resources
- Human resources
- Information or information systems

Ask yourself, based upon what you know about your mission and how you have chosen to compete, what level of capability you need in each of these areas to be successful. What level of capability do you currently have? And what will it cost to add capability you are missing?

Assessment of Return/Profit

Having completed your analysis to this point, you are now ready to complete the numbers/financial section of your plan. You know your "ideal" customer. Now think about the size of your customer base. How big is it? Is it growing or shrinking? You know your competition and potential competition. What share of the market are they likely to consume? What share can you hope to retain or take from them? You know the key capabilities you will need to carry out your plan. What will it cost you to acquire and retain these capabilities? As you are working these numbers, prepare three scenarios: your best-case assumptions; your worst-case assumptions; something in between. Then review the results. If your worst-case assumptions won't generate the minimum profit, cash flow, and return on investment you need, then you must rethink your strategy or, at a minimum, develop a contingency plan. What would you do if the worst case happened?

Plan for Communicating and Implementing Your Strategy

Up to this point, you have developed a plan. But it is only a plan. It is only wishful thinking unless you take action. To ensure that you do take action, you need a list of things to do. One thing you must do is communicate your plan to your employees. At a minimum, you need to prepare a summary of your business strategy you can distribute to your employees and hold a meeting with your employees and discuss your business strategy. Once you have communicated your strategy to your employees, your next step should be to draw up a plan for implementing that strategy. Your implementation plan should be a written list of what needs to be done, who will do it, and by when the task will be completed. For example, you may have identified a new technology as a key capability you must have to carry out your strategy. How are you going to obtain that technology? Who will contact vendors? Who will secure financing? By when will these steps be completed? In developing this implementation plan, involve your people. Call a meeting and say: "The last time we met, I reviewed our business strategy. Now we have to decide how we will implement that strategy. And I need your ideas." Brainstorm with them the actions you need to take. They'll go out of the room with a clear idea of what needs to be done to make your business a success. More important, because you involved them in the process, they will be personally committed to action!

__2__

How to Hire

One of the most important decisions you must make as a business owner is whom to hire. The people you employ can make or break your business. But you must recognize that you will never be able to hire the best people—only the best *available* people. You are always limited to the people who apply for the position you have open. Given that your choice will always be limited, how do you hire the best available person? Here are some helpful suggestions:

Make your search for job candidates
a continuous process.

Start your search for employees as far in advance as you can. Don't wait until you're so desperate that you hire the first applicant who walks in the door. Be on the lookout for potential candidates constantly, even if you have no job openings at the moment. When somebody who's looking for a job walks in the door or sends you a letter, take the time to consider their application. If they look promising, go ahead with an interview. Sure, you'll be investing precious time in considering an application when you have no immediate plans to hire. But think of it this way—you are investing in the future.

Obviously, you need to tell such job candidates what you are doing. Make it clear that you have no jobs open at the moment, but wanted to talk to them in case something became available in the future. Ask them if you can keep their names on file. This way, when you do have a job opening, you can contact these prescreened applicants. True, many of them will have other jobs by then and may no longer be interested in making a change. Yet many will—particularly those who had a strong desire to work for your company in the first place. And after all, isn't that the kind of person you really want to hire—someone who really wants to work for you?

Use part-time, temporary, and/or seasonal employment as a low-risk tryout.

Observing a person's performance on a limited trial basis, as a temporary, part-time, or seasonal employee, is a great way to find out what kind of full-time employee he or she might be. If it doesn't work out, you haven't lost anything. If such an employee does the job well, you have a proven candidate for the next full-time job available.

Another good idea is to hire temporary workers to supplement the regular work force during peak periods or to fill in for regular employees who are on leave or on vacation. Obviously, some people are interested only in part-time, seasonal, or temporary work; they don't want to work full time. Many others, however, use part-time or temporary jobs to break into the work force for the first time, to move to a new line of work, or to support themselves while they look for full-time jobs in your company. The limited or trial work period gives them a chance to get to know you and gives you a chance to get to know them.

Use the "success indicators" to hire the best available person.

Remember that any person's potential for success in a given job is a function of all the following success indicators:

- Their job knowledge (the "how to" factor)
- Their motivation (the "want to" factor)
- Their ability (the "able to" factor)

Job knowledge is determined by a candidate's education, training, and experience. Ideally, you are looking for people who already know how to do the job you'll be asking them to do and have done it successfully in the not-too-distant past. To evaluate job knowledge, check each candidate's work history, training, and education. Ask candidates what they have done, where they did it, and how well they did it. Ask about their successes and the problems they've faced. Ask about their training and education as it applies to the job you are trying to fill.

Ask for references, and call them to find out what kind of work the applicant did and how well he or she did it. Also, verify training and education. Did the person really obtain the degree, complete the course, and so on? Unfortunately, you can't depend entirely on what applicants tell you about their education, training, and experience, since many people will exaggerate and a few may even lie. At minimum, you should verify the dates of employment, training, and education with third-party sources.

Internal motivation is determined by what the candidate gets from performing the job. Think of work performance as an exchange—the candidate will perform the job well if he receives something he wants in return. Obviously, money is one thing the candidate wants. But money is rarely the only thing—and often not the most important thing—that people want from a job. There are a lot of ways people can make money. Excellent job performance is usually motivated by something that goes beyond salary. For whatever reason, the best employees are those who enjoy what they do. Maybe they like the hours; maybe it's the location; maybe it's the people they work with; maybe it's the work itself. We all want and like different things. Your task is to make the best match—to find a person who wants to do and likes to do the job you're hiring them for.

How do you find out what job applicants want and like? Ask them. Knowing about their hobbies and interests can help you decide if they would be good at a particular job. For example, a person who likes to shop may enjoy retail sales. Someone who likes outdoor sports may also like working outdoors, selling sports equipment, or coaching. You should also find out what the candidate liked (and disliked) about jobs he or she held in the past.

If a candidate hated working overtime on a previous job, you wouldn't want to hire him or her for a job that requires a lot of overtime. If he or she hated commuting long distances to a previous job, you may be able to offer a place to work closer to home.

Try to find out why applicants want to work for you. Are they just looking for a job—any job—or are they attracted to your particular company for some reason? Get a sense of what the candidates think it would be like to do the job you will be asking them to do. Find out what their goals and ambitions are. Spend some time getting to know them. Then ask yourself if it's realistic to expect that they'll get what they want from the job you have to offer. If they will, great! You've got a prime candidate. If not, think twice. By offering the person a job, you may create a situation that will make both of you unhappy.

Finally, consider each applicant's natural ability. Excellent performers are often excellent because they were born with or developed unique traits that are ideally matched to their jobs. Consider the job you are attempting to fill. Does it require any particular personal characteristics—for instance, physical strength, hand/eye coordination, or verbal ability? What type of personality does best on that job—quiet and introspective, or boisterous and outgoing? How is the candidate similar to or different from people you know who currently perform that type of job well?

How do you evaluate a job candidate's mental and physical abilities? Testing is one option, but testing can be expensive, time consuming, and all too frequently unreliable. Your best bet may be simply talking to the candidates and drawing your own conclusions. It's also a good idea to observe applicants performing some of the duties they would have on the job. For example, in hiring trainers for our own company, we have prospective candidates prepare and lead a short training session. Their performance is never perfect, but the session allows us to form some opinion of their training skills.

When you're through with interviews, reference checks, and testing, you should have a clear idea of the "success indicators" for each candidate. Then, and only then, are you prepared to make your selection. The ideal choice would be a person with all the requisite job knowledge, the necessary abilities, and a strong inner drive or motivation to do the work. However, the chances of finding such a perfect match are slim. Remember, you're selecting the best available, not necessarily the best. It's unlikely that any candidate will rate a perfect "10" on all three success indicators, so you must choose the candidate with the best combination of traits across all three indicators. For example, the best person to hire might be a candidate who doesn't have the ideal mental or physical traits for the job, but has a strong drive to succeed and excellent job knowledge. Never discount a candidate for weaknesses in one of the three areas; strengths in the other areas can easily outweigh any weaknesses.

We have found that job knowledge, motivation, and ability are roughly equal predictors of job performance, with motivation having a slight edge. Your task in selecting a candidate is to evaluate what you have learned about their job knowledge, motivation, and abilities. How successful do you think they will be in the job? If you have any doubts, don't hire them, at least not until you resolve your doubts. A critical factor in the performance of any new employee is your belief that the person will succeed. To hire an employee for whom you have lesser expectations is to court disaster.

___3___

Finding People to Work for You

A recent report of the National Institute of Business Management predicts that labor shortages will worsen rapidly in the 1990s. Who will be hardest hit by increased competition for workers? You guessed it—small businesses. The reasons for an impending nation-wide shortage of workers are both demographic and economic. The work force that has been growing at the rate of 3 percent per year is expected to grow at the rate of only 1 percent per year in the next decade (the slowest growth rate since the 1930s) due to the influx of the "baby bust" generation, those born in the early 1970s. Many of these young people entering the work force will have poor education and limited skills. Don't be surprised if many can't read or write. The long and short of our "labor crisis" is that attracting and retaining good workers will be increasingly difficult in the future. If you own or operate a small business and you don't want to be stuck with hiring illiterates (if you can find anyone to work at all) or paying two to three times the minimum wage to attract young workers to entry-level jobs, you should take steps now to expand the pool of applicants for jobs with your company. You should also adopt personnel policies and practices to make your business a "good place to work" so that you can retain your best employees.

One way to expand the pool of applicants for positions in your business is to offer prospective employees an alternative to a stan-dard eight-hour-per-day, forty-hour-per-week job. Many older workers and adult women with young children who might not otherwise apply for a full-time forty-hour-a-week, eight-hour-a-day job may be attracted to your business if you can offer them more control over their working hours. Obviously, making part-time work available is an alternative. But suppose your business is such that you can't survive with just part-time workers? Here are some alternatives that allow you to have "full-time" employees while still offering your workers more control over their working hours. Innovative work arrangements may allow you to attract capable workers with good skills and a strong work ethic who might not otherwise apply for positions with your company.

Job Sharing

With job sharing, two employees share the same job and job responsibilities. One might work in the mornings and one in the afternoons. Or one might work from Monday through Wednesday morning while the other takes Wednesday afternoon through Friday. Or the two employees might rotate the number of days they work each week. For example, employee A works two days the first week and three the next while employee B works three days the first week and two the next. Regardless of the arrangement, you have someone occupying the position a full forty hours every week while the employees who share the position each get to work only half-time. In addition to being able to offer what is really part-time work for a full-time job (and therefore attract applicants who might not be interested in full-time work), there are several other advantages for your business that can occur as a result of job sharing. First, with two employees working the position, a "fresh" person is always available—there is no afternoon or end-of-the-week letdown in performance. Second, since the two employees are normally only working twenty hours per week, they may be much more willing than a regular forty-hour-per-week employee to work more than their normal hours in periods of peak work loads. Finally, with two employees working the same job, you have a built-in, fully trained replacement who might be willing to work a full-time schedule on a temporary basis, should one of the two go on vacation or be out due to sickness or for personal reasons.

If you do decide to provide job sharing as an alternative work arrangement, recognize that filling such a position is more complicated than hiring someone for a regular full-time job. In job sharing, two people are involved, and they must be compatible. Matching a "neatnik" with someone who thrives in clutter just won't work. You'll have nothing but continuous arguments. In addition, job sharing places an increased demand on the employees involved to communicate and coordinate their activities. They must leave messages for each other about the status of projects or work activities; agree upon one standard system for organizing work so the job-sharing partner can find what he or she needs; and decide who will perform periodic functions such as end-of-the-day or end-of-the-week reporting or record keeping. An additional issue you must resolve is how you will handle benefits such as life insurance, health insurance, sick pay, and vacations/holidays. If you provide such benefits for job-sharing employees (and most companies with job sharing do), then you must decide whether full benefits will be provided to both employees or split between the two the way pay and working hours are split.

Job Splitting

Job splitting is an alternative to job sharing that retains many of the benefits of job sharing while minimizing the amount of communication and coordination required between the two employees. Essentially, with job splitting two employees share the same job, but duties and responsibilities of the job are "split" rather than just the hours. With job splitting, you are dividing one full-time position into two distinct parts. The division may be according to when the work must be performed—for example, morning or afternoon, first of the week or end of the week. Or, and more likely, the division can be by job function or skills required. The advantage of this latter approach is that you can seek out persons with skills more closely matched to the specific job requirements or you can allow the two employees who will be splitting the job to divide up the job functions according to their own preferences and skills.

Flextime

Job sharing and job splitting involve two employees dividing up one full-time job so each employee can work part time while the company retains the benefits of a full-time employee. Under flextime, employees work a full forty-hour week (or eighty hours over a period of two weeks), but gain some degree of control over their starting and ending time. Normally, under flextime the company adopts a "core" time when all employees must be at work—for example, 9:00 A.M. to 3:00 P.M. However, employees are allowed to adjust their starting and ending time around those core hours. For example, one employee might come in at 6:30 and leave at 3:00 while another might come in at 9:30 and leave at 6:00. Under flextime, the only requirements are that all employees work their full eight hours and that they are present during the core hours. Additionally, under some flextime plans, employees are allowed to "bank" hours. Thus, an employee who wanted a half-day off with pay could work twelve hours one day and only four hours the next. The advantage of flextime for employees is that they can adjust their working hours to meet their own personal needs and desires. Morning people can come in early. Night people can sleep late. Employees with children have a few extra hours to get them off to school in the morning or can arrange their work hours so they can be home before their children in the afternoons. In addition to advantages for employees, flextime also has at least one advantage for your business. With some employees coming in early and others staying late, you can extend the hours your business is open and serve customers earlier in the morning and later in the afternoon without having to pay for overtime.

As in the case of other alternative work schedules, flextime does present some issues you have to resolve. For example, how will you provide supervision over the longer workday? Your alternatives are to provide no supervision during certain hours, split the workday with an assistant manager so a manager is always present, or make one of the employees coming in early and one staying late acting supervisor during the non-core hours. A second issue you will encounter with flextime is how to keep track of the hours employees actually work. You can place employees on their honor to work their full eight hours; install a time clock and have employees clock in and out; or create a sign-in/sign-out sheet where employees record their time of arrival and departure. A third flextime issue is how much freedom employees will have to set their own hours. For example, will they be able to change their working hours daily (i.e., no one is tardy until core time begins) or only periodically (i.e., once a month, once a quarter, etc.)? A frequent problem with flextime is that many employees may elect to come in early. Consequently, you may find yourself with less coverage in the late afternoon. To avoid such a problem, it may be necessary for you to restrict the number of employees who can come in early and require employees to rotate their hours periodically to give everyone who desires it a chance at the early arrival time.

Compressed Workweek

A compressed workweek is similar to flextime in that it gives employees the ability to work a full-time job while still having time off during the normal workweek (Monday through Friday) to take care of personal business. Under a compressed workweek, employees may be allowed to work four ten-hour days; three twelve-hour days; or alternate weeks working four nine-hour days one week and five nine-hour days the next. Thus, employees get one to two days off every week or every two weeks. For your company, longer workdays may mean that you can make more efficient use of equipment (for example, your delivery trucks stay out an extra hour or two each day) and/or extend your business hours during most days of the week. Compressed workweeks also have the advantage of typically reducing absenteeism, since employees have time to take care of personal business such as routine doctor/dentist appointments, and employees soon recognize that a nonpaid absence costs them not just eight hours' pay, but ten or twelve hours' pay. The main disadvantage of adopting a compressed workweek is that by doing so you place your company on a work schedule at odds with other businesses and what customers have come to expect. Your competitors are probably on a five-day week (or even six- or seven-day week), while your business would be on a shorter workweek. One way to overcome this limitation is to vary the days of the week your employees work. For example, some might work a compressed workweek that begins on Monday and ends on Thursday while others work a Tuesday through Friday or Wednesday through Saturday schedule. If you can tolerate a reduced staff during certain days of the week (for example, those days of the week when sales are slow), a compressed workweek provides your employees with a flexible work schedule and allows you to increase staffing and have your business open for longer hours on those days when you are likely to have the most customers.

The key to making alternative work schedules work for your business is to match your business needs and staffing requirements with the needs and desires of a pool of workers you are trying to attract. With the shrinking supply of qualified young workers to fill entry-level positions in your business, you need to find creative alternatives to the standard forty-hour-per-week, eight-hour-per-day, nine-to-five job. No longer will it be enough just to place a sign in your shop window to attract the work force your business requires. In the next decade, "good" workers will be in great demand. To compete in a tight labor market, you will need to make your business a "good place to work." One way to do that is to offer your employees an alternative work schedule. Such a schedule meets an increasing need of the workers of tomorrow— the ability to exercise more control over their working hours.

4

How to Train the People Who Work for You

Training the people who work for you is critical if you intend to keep your business strong. If you do not have a knowledgeable work force, the job just will not get done—not the right way and not on time. Most businesses recognize the importance of training. Maybe that is why so much money is spent on training. From recent estimates, businesses with one to nine employees spend over $360 million a year on training. Businesses with ten to forty-nine employees spend over one billion dollars per year. Training in the United States in the 1980s was an $8 billion-per-year business. And that just counts actual outlays for purchased training programs. It does not include in-house programs or the cost of on-the-job training. If all the other types of training are included along with travel costs, statistics, per diem, and so on, the total spent on training approaches is not $8 billion, but nearly $30 billion for U.S. firms alone.

These numbers sound staggering—and they are. But they gain even greater significance when we realize that most of these dollars spent on training are wasted. By some estimates, employees who attend training—even the best and most professionally designed training—absorb just 15 percent of what is presented in the program, and apply only 15 percent of that 15 percent. That is a tremendous loss. But it is not only the loss of training dollars. A much larger potential loss to your company is from the mistakes new—and even seasoned—employees can make if they are inadequately trained. Andrew Grove, president of Intel Corporation—the microprocessor and computer memory device company—and author of *High Output Management,* told the following story in the January 27, 1984, issue of *Fortune* magazine. He says in that piece:

> The consequences of an employee being insufficiently trained can be much more serious. In an instance at Intel, for example, one of our sophisticated pieces of production machinery in a silicon fabrication plant—a machine called an ion implanter— drifted slightly out of tune. The machine operator . . . was relatively new. While she was trained in the basic skills needed to operate the machine, she hadn't been taught to recognize the signs of an out-of-tune condition. So she continued to operate the machine, subjecting nearly a day's worth of almost completely processed silicon wafers to the wrong machine conditions. By the time the situation was discovered, material worth more than $1 million had passed through the machine— and had to be scrapped. Because it takes over two weeks to make up such a loss with fresh material, deliveries to our customers slipped, compounding the problem.

If the potential loss from poorly trained employees is so great, how do you effectively train your employees? How do you avoid wasting time and money on training that does not take? How do you ensure that your work force is a truly knowledgeable one? Here are some suggestions.

Provide the Right Training

Make sure the training you provide is the training your employees really need. A significant portion of the training dollars and the time devoted to training is wasted because it is spent on the wrong thing. Training—as opposed to education, which we will discuss later—should be directed specifically toward providing employees with skills they do not currently have, but must have to perform. In effect, the appropriateness of any given training is a function of two things: the need for a skill and the absence of a skill. Much training is wasted because the employee either already possesses the skill(s), thus does not need the training, and/or does not possess the skill(s) but has no immediate need for the skill(s) anyway—the absence of the skill does not matter for performance, or, more likely, the skill is not immediately required for performance on the job.

To make sure the training you provide is the training your employees really need, you should first complete a training needs assessment. There are two parts to such an assessment. First, you identify the skills your employees require to meet the needs of your customers, and second, you match your employees with the skills you have identified. Let's examine both of these steps.

Step 1: What skills do your employees require?

An employee who possesses a skill is an employee who can properly execute behaviors required to satisfy the needs of a customer. A "behavior" is something a person does or says; therefore your first task in identifying training needs for your employees is to list all the things they must do or say to satisfy your customers. To make your list, just take a blank sheet of paper and start listing items as they come to you. Don't worry about the order or, at this point, which employee needs the skill—the ability to demonstrate the behavior.

As you make your list, certain obvious skills will come to mind:

- Answer the phone.
- Take an order.
- Complete an order form.
- Locate a part in a catalog.
- Locate an item in inventory.
- Operate the cash register.
- Make change.
- Complete a credit card order.
- Complete a credit card application.
- Estimate a job.

And so on.

But don't stop with the obvious. Keep adding to your list. What about:

- Answer a customer's question about how to do something.
- Make a customer feel important, respected, and comfortable with a transaction.
- Report a problem.
- Make a suggestion.

You need to draw up as exhaustive a list of skills (behaviors) as you can. If you have a partner or existing employees, ask for their suggestions about skills to add. Your first task is to develop a complete skills inventory.

Step 2: Match your skills inventory to specific employees.

As you are developing your skills inventory, you are not matching skills to employees. Once you have compiled your skills inventory, your job then is to decide who needs each particular skill. Not all employees do. You need to ask yourself two questions to make the correct match between employee and skill. First, if taught this skill, would the employee be able to (need to) apply the skill immediately after training on the job? The opportunity to immediately apply the skill is critical. We all have short memories; or, more precisely, many thoughts, ideas, concepts, and so on compete for our attention. Consequently, if we learn a skill but do not immediately apply the skill, it is crowded out of our memory by the thousands of other sights, symbols, thoughts, ideas, and other information we are bombarded with every day. Repetition is the only method for ensuring, for most of us, that something learned is remembered. And repetition is dependent upon application—immediate application. Never train a person in a skill unless they will have the opportunity to apply what they learn from the training immediately on the job.

A second question to ask in matching employees to skills is this: Do they already possess the skill? Have they done it before, or, in the words of Robert Mager and Peter Piper, in *Analyzing Performance Problems,* "Could they do it if their life depended on it?" It may sound simple to say that we should not train people on things they already know how to do, but too often training is wasted for exactly that reason. We see an employee who is not performing, and immediately decide that the answer is training. Yet the reason for poor performance or nonperformance has nothing to do with a lack of knowledge or skill. The employee could do it, has done it before, but is just not doing it. In later chapters we will discuss how to respond to a "won't do" (nontraining) problem, as Mager and Piper refer to it, as opposed to a "can't do" (training) problem. When matching people to training, just be sure that the cause of nonperformance is a "can't do" problem.

The Five Steps to Training Success

If you developed a skills inventory and matched these skills to employees according to need, you have a good start on developing an effective training program. You might deliver this training yourself, or you might hire others to deliver it. Regardless of how the training is delivered, the sequence in which your employees are taught new skills will have much to do with the success of the training. Therefore, it is not sufficient to just identify the skills your employees require, and match people to these skills. You have to make sure they are trained in the right way.

Of all the discussions on training we have seen, perhaps the best was presented by Thomas F. Gilbert in his book, *Human Competence: Engineering Worthy Performance.* Gilbert suggests a sequence of five steps you should follow that are most likely to lead to training success. In summary, here are Gilbert's five steps.

Step 1: Motivate and Familiarize

Unfortunately, we often begin the process of teaching people a new skill with the assumption that they are interested in learning the skill, and see the need for the skill to the same extent as we do. We are often wrong in this assumption. Therefore, Gilbert suggests that your first step in teaching a new skill is to create "a need to know."

Why is the skill important? What difference does it make whether or not one possesses the skill? For most people, the acquisition of a new skill requires time, effort, and expenditure of energy. Old, comfortable modes of behavior may have to be put aside so that new behavior can be learned. New methods, new techniques, and new modes of behavior are required. At first, these new methods, new techniques, and new methods of behavior are uncomfortable and unnatural. Learning a new skill requires change, and change is difficult. None of us will change until we see a reason to do so. Your first step in teaching a new skill should then be to create that need for change.

In our consulting business, we spend most of our time teaching executives, managers, and supervisors new management skills. We teach participative management, where the manager/supervisor acts as a coach and facilitator rather than decision maker and problem solver. For most of the people we train, this new style of management is significantly different from any they have practiced or experienced before. Adapting to this new style requires a drastic change for most of them; therefore we begin our training with an exercise to help them reach their own conclusions about the need to change—the need to learn these new management skills. Our exercise is simple. We ask managers and supervisors to compare and contrast the 1950s, 1960s, 1970s, and 1980s in areas such as politics, economics, family life, competitiveness, and work force. The new management style we teach is designed to address the needs of the business climate of the 1980s and 1990s. Upon completion of our exercise, most of our trainees have confirmed for themselves what they already knew—the world of work, the world of business is drastically different from the world of three decades ago, or even two decades ago. New styles of management are required to meet the economic, social, political, environmental, and other changes that have occurred. There is a need to change the way we manage. The purpose of our exercise is to allow the managers and supervisors we train to reach their own conclusion about their need to learn new skills.

Regardless of what skill you wish your employees to acquire

from the training you offer, like ours, your first task is to enable them to see a need to change—a need to learn and apply the new skills. Start your training with the consequences of failing to possess the skill. Make sure you have a good answer to the question any person you train is likely to ask (or think of asking): "Why do I need to know this?" If possible, arrange for those you are training to arrive at the conclusion that they "need to know" themselves.

Step 2: Check People Out on the Basic Skill Required for Learning the New Skill

Certain basic skills are a prerequisite to learning other skills. For example, unless I know how to add and subtract, I cannot learn how to balance a checkbook. Unless I have basic knowledge about the operation of an internal combustion engine, I cannot be taught to make repairs to that engine. In your screening of applicants, you should have checked for basic knowledge and skills employees brought to the job as a result of prior education, training, or experience. They should know the basics, but check them out anyway. Maybe a brief refresher is in order.

Step 3: Teach the Specific Skills of the Task

With mastery of the basic skills, your employees are now ready to learn specific skills. Here, we refer to the normal, usual, or typical. How does an employee fill the typical order? What steps should be followed in making common repairs? What is the one way that works most of the time? For example, 90 percent of the time, customers order standard quantities of items from the standard catalog. First, teach employees how to fill that standard order.

Step 4: Teach Mastery Skills

Once your employees have learned to fill the standard or typical order, they are ready to progress to the atypical or complex—the exception to the rule. Once they learn to make the common type of repair, they are now ready to advance to the more complex.

Step 5: Provide an Opportunity for Immediate Application

Finally, whatever skill you teach, arrange for your employees to apply/use the new skill on the job immediately after the completion of training. Of all our suggestions about how to make training effective, application—immediate application—is probably most important. You can run exercises during training. You can try to create realistic scenarios. But nothing is as effective to cement what people have learned as to send them out of the training into the store—or office—to apply the skill in a real life—real customer—situation. In our own training programs, we provide immediate follow-up application of all we teach. It is perhaps the most important thing we do in teaching new skills.

Other Keys to Training Success

If you follow the "Five Steps to Training Success" discussed previously, you have a good chance of creating a skilled work force. Here are some more suggestions for making your training stick.

Use Memory Aids

It is very human for us to forget rules, numbers, sequences, steps, and so on. There is just so much competition—so many things to remember. What we need is an aid—a way of relating what we already know to something new or a rhyme to fix the rule in memory. For example, remember this from school—"i" before "e" except after "c," or when sounded as "a" as in *neighbor* or *weigh*. That is a short, simple aid to memory. Watch your television tonight, you will probably see an advertisement something like this, "Need money? Call 1-800-NEW-LOAN." These are nothing more than associations—ways to remember. Any time you are trying to teach something that must be remembered—a sequence of steps, a number, a rule to follow, and so on—try to find a memory aid. Make up a rhyme, spell out a word, or associate the new with something already known. Any of these will aid memory.

Use the Rule of "5 to 9"

A tremendous amount of research has been conducted on the ability of the average person to remember and recall sequences of numbers. The results of this research are fairly consistent—most people can effectively remember a sequence of no more than five to nine numbers. Longer sequences must be broken down into segments to aid memory. Applications of this "5 to 9" rule are very common. For example, look at your telephone number: three-digit area code, three-digit prefix, and four-digit number. Most people can learn and remember a telephone number because it is broken into short sequences of five or fewer numbers. The same is true of social security numbers and many other sequences people need to remember.

Provide a Job Aid

Any time you must teach people to execute a sequence of steps in a particular order, especially if the sequence is long, complex, and/or will not be executed frequently, provide a job aid. In its simplest form, a job aid is nothing more than the list of steps in the proper sequence—perhaps a checklist. A pilot's preflight checklist is a job aid. Forms that employees complete in the performance of a task or transaction can also serve as job aids, as can prompts on a computer screen. In our training, we teach managers and supervisors to conduct meetings with their employees following a carefully designed agenda. To help them prepare and conduct these meetings, we provide a simple one-page form. The form serves not only as a record of the meeting (when completed, the form provides a summary of the minutes) but also as a memory aid for the manager/supervisor conducting the meeting to ensure that every item is covered, *and* covered in the right sequence.

Teach People to Encode, and Decoding Will Follow

Suppose an employee needs to know how to read an order form (decode), and how to complete an order form (encode). Which skill do you teach first—reading or completing? The answer is completing (encoding). The reason for this is that once a person learns to complete the form correctly (encode), he or she is likely also to learn simultaneously to read the form (decode). You have taught two skills at the same time. Even if the person may never be required to actually complete the form (or make a drawing, etc.), it may be better to teach him or her to do so. If you do, a better understanding of the form's content is likely to follow. (This is one exception to the rule that you should not teach a skill that employees will not use immediately.)

Your Responsibility for Education

So far in this chapter, we have discussed your responsibility for training—providing your employees with the skills they require to meet the needs of your customers. We close this chapter with reference to your other responsibility—the education of your work force and potential work force.

Training your work force and educating your work force are equally vital but significantly different undertakings. Training provides specific skills required for performance on the job. Education provides basic skills and enhances the person's capability. Fredrick Harmon and Garry Jacobs, in *The Vital Differences,* express the difference between training and education this way:

Whatever a person's inherent capacities, training improves the level of skills available for expressing those capacities; but education increases the level of capacity itself. Training refines the tools of expression; education improves the person.

Education trains the mind to consider many possibilities, to see things from a new and wider perspective, to question and challenge the status quo, to think and imagine, to innovate and invent, to make decisions for oneself, and to act on one's initiative.

Not only the training but also the education of your work force is vital to the success of your business. Without an educated population to draw from, you will not be able to hire the quality work force you must have for your business to survive. And today in the United States, that educated population is not being provided. You undoubtedly discovered this as you attempted to hire people to fill your vacancies. You likely found some of the following:

- Applicants who could barely read or write
- Applicants who could not write a simple letter or fill out an application form
- Applicants whose math skills, and perhaps verbal skills, were barely minimum

You are not alone. Here are some shocking statistics cited by Jack Grayson, the founder of the American Productivity & Quality Center, and Carla O'Dell in their book, *American Business: A Two Minute Warning:*

- Ninety percent of Japanese youth finish high school as against about 75 percent in the United States.
- Today, 27 million Americans, or more, are functionally illiterate, more than the entire population of Canada; 15 million of the functionally illiterate are at work.
- A bank in the Midwest found that half of the high school graduates it hired could not pass a simple math test.
- At GM, about 15 percent of hourly employees are functionally illiterate.

There are many complex reasons why American educational institutions are failing to provide a knowledgeable work force. Yet there is very little disagreement that American schools are failing in their primary task—to produce literate, disciplined, and competent workers.

So what is your role—your responsibility—in responding to this failure of American education? Regardless of your political persuasion, it is vitally important that you get involved with other federal, state, and local government, education, and business leaders to find an answer. Take an active interest in promoting the quality of your state and local educational institutions. You will be glad you did. These institutions have a major role in providing your work force with the basic skills they will need to help you keep your business strong.

__5__

Paying for Performance

Traditionally in this country, we have paid most employees a straight hourly wage or an annual salary. Employees got paid the same amount whether or not the company was profitable. More important, they got paid the same, or nearly the same, regardless of how hard they worked. Additionally, employees came to expect annual increases in their base pay either as a cost of living increase and/or as an increase based upon their time with the company. We might vary the increase a small amount based upon performance so that the high performers got slightly more, but everyone got approximately the same percentage increase with just a few percentage points separating the high and low performers. Some of us had a bonus system for providing an additional reward to our high performers. But the bonuses we paid rarely amounted to very much as a percentage of total compensation. In effect, most employees in the same job get paid pretty much the same and receive approximately the same increase each year. What's wrong with that? Plenty.

The major disadvantage of our traditional compensation practices is that, for most employees, base pay has lost any relationship to performance. Our employees have learned that they will make the same whether they work hard or take it easy. Consequently, most people don't work as hard as they could. In fact, in a variety of surveys conducted throughout the 1970s and 1980s, American workers were asked whether they worked as hard as they could. In practically every survey, workers said they didn't. When asked why, they replied, "Because all the benefits of their hard work went to managers and owners, not to employees." In short, American workers don't believe it "pays" to work harder.

A second problem with our traditional approach to compensation is that our employees now expect regular annual increases in their base pay. Additionally, they expect these increases to average 5 percent or better. At a minimum, they expect equal or slightly better than the "expected percentage increase in wages" they read about in the local newspaper. As long as the business climate was such that you could pass along these increases to your customers in the form of price increases, you could afford to grant employees the extra pay. But if your company is like most today, not only can you not increase your prices, you are looking for ways to cut costs and/or prices. If you grant wage increases without offsetting increases in productivity, quality improvement, etc., and you can't pass along these increased costs, you have a significant problem. As little as a 5 percent annual increase would increase your direct labor cost by over 60 percent in just ten years and more than double it within fifteen years. And that doesn't include the impact such increases would have on benefits you may be paying that are tied to base wages. These would go up also. It is not hard to see how your labor costs could skyrocket in just a few years.

How then do you get out of this dilemma? Is it possible for you to offer your employees the potential for high total earnings while still holding down your operating cost? Yes, it is. But you have to go beyond base wages to create a total compensation system. Today, most authorities think such a system should consist of some or all of the following:

1. Base wages
2. "Lump sum payments" instead of annual percentage increases
3. Group incentive bonuses
4. Profit-sharing
5. Pay-for-knowledge
6. Employee stock ownership

We will examine each of these and how they might fit into your total compensation strategy.

Base Pay

Earlier, we said that most American workers no longer saw a direct relationship between their base pay and their performance. In fact, for most workers there is very little relationship, since most workers in the same job get paid about the same. When an employee doesn't see a relationship between his or her behavior and an offered reward, the reward is not motivating. As a result, for most employees, their base pay is not motivating. Sure, if you offer an employee a 20 percent increase provided his performance improves, his performance might improve *until he gets the raise*. However, once he finally gets the raise, don't expect his higher level of performance to continue. How many times have you seen average or just "okay" performers blossom just before their annual review only to return to their old selves once the review was over?

If the base wages you pay employees don't motivate them to high performance, what do you get for the wages you are paying? You get them to come to work for you (to show up most of the time) and you get minimum performance (high enough so they will not be fired). It's sad, but that is all you can expect. Since that is all you can expect, you should adjust your base compensation strategy accordingly.

The base wages you pay and annual increase you offer should be the minimum you must pay to attract and retain the basic talent you need. Your objective in setting base pay rates should be to compete in your labor market for employees. You must offer base compensation that is equal to or almost equal to that offered by competing businesses in your geographical area. You don't want to be the highest-paying employer, since high pay (base pay) is not going to guarantee you high performance. Neither do you want to be the lowest-paying employer, since you want to be able to attract the basic talent you need. It is much better to be near, but slightly below, the average for your area. How do you determine the average? First, you should clearly define the job you are filling. What are the education, training, skill, and other requirements for the various jobs you offer? Then check salary surveys for your area. Thousands of such surveys are conducted throughout the U.S. each year. To find a survey covering your type of business and your area, try contacting the following:

- The U.S. Department of Labor
- Compensation consultants
- Your trade or professional association
- The Chamber of Commerce
- Employment agencies

Chances are, one or more of these sources can lead you to a recent salary survey that is right for you. Also, check published reports of salaries in trade magazines, newsletters, and in your local papers.

When you locate a survey, obtain a copy and check to see what comparable jobs are paying. You should note not only the average pay, but also the low and the high pay for that job in each survey. Also, check the age and tenure of employees and turnover data for companies included in the survey. Age and tenure information is important since companies with a younger or newer work force may be paying lower rates because they have many people in entry-level positions. Turnover data is important because a high turnover figure might signal that these companies are losing employees due to low wages. Finally, check more than one survey. Surveys vary greatly in accuracy, number of companies covered, etc. Some are notorious for undervaluing jobs, while others go to the opposite extreme. Use these surveys as a guide only. Just because the wage data are reported to the nearest penny doesn't mean they are accurate.

Lump Sum Payments

If you carefully monitor survey data, you should be able to keep your base pay rates within reason. But how do you avoid having your base rates creep out of line as a result of annual increases? You do that by substituting lump sum payments for some of the annual increases. A lump sum payment is a one-time cash payment equal to some percentage of base wages. For example, instead of giving a 4 percent annual increase, you give your employees a one-time cash payment equal to 5 percent of their annual pay. The chief advantage of a lump sum payment over an annual increase is that, unlike an annual increase, it doesn't accumulate. You are not adding the 5 percent payment on each year in the future. The advantage for employees is that they get the payment all at once as one large check instead of having it spread out over the year.

Group Incentive Bonuses

Neither base pay nor lump sum payments are motivating. Group incentive bonuses are. Consequently, a major component of your compensation strategy should be to provide an opportunity for your employees to make substantial bonuses, provided their performance improves. One of the most popular group incentives being adopted by large and small companies over the last five years is called gain sharing.

As its name implies, gainsharing is an incentive program whereby employees share in financial gains that come to their company as a result of their efforts. A formula for calculating gains is developed and then performance each month or quarter is compared to performance during some historical period or to some target performance. If current performance is better than the historical or target base, then a gain is made and the company and employees split the gain. Employees receive cash bonus payments in a separate check. In a manufacturing environment, the formula will often compare direct labor costs to the sales value of production. In short, if employees produce more for lower labor costs, then a gain is made and a bonus is paid. In a service environment, employees might have targets or goals to meet on a variety of measures (such as customer satisfaction, service delivery times, and/or operating costs). If they perform better than the targets, then they earn bonus points that are worth so much in cash.

Gainsharing has been used in the United States since the 1930s and has been extremely successful. For example, 80 percent of the companies adopting gainsharing have said it had a positive or very positive impact on performance (productivity, cost savings, improvement in customer service, and so on). Since gainsharing has been around a long time, a lot of books and articles exist to help you design your own company's gainsharing plan. For example,

Maximum Performance Management, by Joseph H. Boyett and Henry P. Conn, contains detailed information about how to design and install a gainsharing plan. Books and articles will explain standard gainsharing formulas that other companies have used and will point out other decisions you must make in designing a plan. Since there are some legal ramifications of gainsharing, such as ensuring compliance with the Fair Labor Standards Act, you should read some of the many books on gainsharing and have any plan reviewed by your accountant and attorney before you adopt it.

Profit-Sharing

Profit-sharing is similar to gain sharing in that employees have the opportunity to earn bonuses based upon company performance. In this case, you set aside a certain percentage (either a fixed amount or adjusted each year) of the profits of the company that will be paid to employees if certain annual profit goals are met or exceeded. Bonuses are paid out in cash, as a contribution to a retirement fund, or partially in cash and partially as a contribution toward retirement. Like gainsharing, profit-sharing has certain legal ramifications and you need to check out any plan with your accountant and attorney.

The advantage of profit-sharing is that it ties any bonuses you pay to the actual profits of the company. Under gainsharing, you conceivably could be paying bonuses even when the company was not profitable or when profit goals weren't met. (The reason for this is that many gainsharing formulas do not include all costs.)

The disadvantage of profit-sharing is that employees may make a bonus even when their performance didn't improve. Maybe the profits occurred because a new product line took off, the business economy improved, or you were able to raise prices. It is likely your employees had little, if anything, to do with these favorable developments. On the other hand, employees could work hard all year and not receive a profit-sharing bonus simply because the economy suffered a downturn, you decided to write off some receivables, or for any number of other reasons out of their control. Finally, profit-sharing bonuses are normally not paid as frequently as gainsharing bonuses. Normally, profits are determined at the end of the year. Thus, employees may work hard all year without any clear assurance they will receive a bonus. You, and they, won't know until the books are closed at year end.

Pay-for-Knowledge

Gainsharing and profit-sharing address your need to establish some link between employee performance and compensation. Since one way employees can improve performance is through teamwork, cooperation, and the willingness to be flexible in job assignments, gainsharing and profit-sharing promote such behavior. But what if employee flexibility is critical to your company? The answer might be to design and install a pay-for-knowledge system.

Under pay-for-knowledge, employees are given the opportunity to earn supplements to their base pay if they can learn and retain skills in a variety of jobs or just increase their skill in one job. The value to your company comes from having multiskilled employees who are willing and able to perform any job you need them to perform. Usually under a pay-for-knowledge system, you define a number of skill sets. Each skill set is worth a certain amount in additional base pay. For example, you might pay an additional fifty cents or one dollar per hour for each skill set an employee learns and can prove he or she retains. As in the case of the other innovative pay systems we have discussed, you need to read more about pay-for-knowledge (*Maximum Performance Management* includes a chapter on this pay system), and you should check out any system you design with your accountant and attorney.

Employee Stock Ownership

Profit-sharing makes it possible for employees to reap financial rewards from the profits of the company. An Employee Stock Ownership Plan (ESOP) allows employees to become part owners in the company. Some people say an ESOP is the biggest gift any employer can give to employees. Undoubtedly it has been, particularly for employees in ESOP companies that became very successful. Many people in the United States have become rich or at least achieved a level of financial security that would have been impossible for them otherwise simply because they were lucky enough to work for an ESOP company. But an ESOP isn't a gift. Employees must earn the shares in the company they receive.

An ESOP can be provided in a public or privately held company. But because of numerous federal laws covering ESOPs, you absolutely must seek professional advice before setting up such a plan. In brief, under an ESOP, your company agrees to make a certain contribution each year in stock or cash to purchase stock to ESOP accounts of employees. The amount of the contribution each year is determined by the owners or board of directors of the company based upon company performance. After a certain number of years of service and/or when they retire, employees receive the stock in their account; they can retain it, sell it back to the company, or (often with certain restrictions) sell it to a third party.

The advantages of an ESOP to employees is that the stock in their account can become extremely valuable if the company does well. The advantage to the company is that it frequently does perform very well once employees realize that they are part owners. If you think about it, this only makes sense. You certainly work hard for your company at least partially because it belongs to you. Your financial future may depend upon your company's success. Why wouldn't most employees respond the same way if they could have some ownership? Obviously, you give up some ownership, but if by your doing so the company is more successful, everyone benefits. Additionally, there may be some significant tax advantages that will flow to you and/or your company from installing an ESOP. Check with your accountant.

These suggestions for how to pay your employees represent new and innovative approaches to employee compensation. Not all of them will be right for your company. And you shouldn't adopt any changes in compensation practices without first doing a considerable amount of research and planning. Do consider what we have suggested, however. You may not be able to get "a fair day's work for a fair day's pay" anymore, but you just might get extraordinary performance from your employees if you are willing to share the financial rewards.

6

Taking the Lead

There is an old saying: "Lead, follow, or get out of the way."
Clearly, you don't intend to follow—that's why you started your
own business. You want to lead for a change. But how do you
know if you are really leading or if you're just getting in the way?
Answering the following four questions will help you find out.

Do you have a clear vision for your company?

Above and beyond anything else, leaders are visionaries. Having
a vision is what separates leaders from followers. What vision do
you have for your company? Imagine your business five or ten
years from now. What comes to mind? Of course, you visualize
the firm growing rapidly and making a lot of money. But your
ultimate vision must be something more than merely making
money. That won't be enough to inspire your employees—even if
you intend to share the wealth with them.

An effective vision is something people rally around because it
is good for customers, employees, the community, investors—
everyone involved in or touched by your business. A vision can
be as grand and far-reaching as the one Martin Luther King ex-
pressed in his famous "I Have A Dream" speech, or as seemingly
ordinary as McDonald's commitment to quality, service, cleanli-
ness, and value.

If you already have a vision of where you want your company

to go, great! If you don't have a vision, you need to develop one. But how?

A useful way to develop a vision is suggested by Jay Conger in his book *The Charismatic Leader*. Conger proposes three basic types of visions applicable to entrepreneurs.

First, you might have a vision for a revolutionary new product or service, such as Edwin Land's idea for instant photography using the Polaroid camera. Could your company offer a product or service with lasting appeal—one that would revolutionize the marketplace? If so, maybe that should be your company's vision.

The second type of vision has a social focus. Maybe the product or service your company offers has a permanent and significant impact on society. That's the type of vision Steven Jobs had for his Next computers. Jobs wanted to produce a computer of particular benefit to educational institutions and revolutionize the learning process.

The third type of vision you might have is more inward-looking. Perhaps you just want to operate your company in a new way. For example, Mary Kay's vision was not only to create a cosmetics business, but to found a company that would offer her female employees the chance to "be all they could be."

The vision you have for your company may encompass more than one of these types. For example, Conger writes, Donald Burr's vision for People Express Airlines incorporated both a social component (making air travel available to those who previously could not afford it) and an inward focus (creating a business that would be managed and operated in a totally new way).

To develop a unique vision for your company, think about these three types of visions. Are any appropriate for what you want to accomplish? Imagine your company five or ten years from now. Will it have revolutionized the marketplace with a new product or service? Helped America deal with some significant social issue or problem?

(NOTE: You may be asking "Didn't Steven Jobs run into trouble with his Next computer and didn't Donald Burr's People Express ultimately fail?" You are right. But the fact that Jobs and Burr ran into trouble with their companies doesn't detract from their visions. Having a good, powerful, motivating vision is important, but it is still no guarantee of success. If it were, the other chapters in this book and even the other sections of this chapter would be unnecessary.)

Can you communicate your vision?

Leaders have to be great communicators. It's one thing to have a vision of the future; it's another to mobilize people to achieve that vision. Leaders motivate people to action through their words.

If you have the gift of oratory, great. But if you're not a naturally talented speaker, does that mean you can't lead? Not at all. The key is to truly believe in your vision and communicate your excitement about it.

The best way to help your employees share your vision is to tell a story illustrating it. How did you arrive at this vision? What event led you to it? Talk about how people's lives might be changed if your vision is realized.

Are you good with the details of execution?

Having and communicating a vision is important. But to realize your vision, you must also know the nuts and bolts of how to get there. A vision is a destination. Leaders have to know the route to follow to reach that destination.

To lead, you must know enough about the details to help your followers plan and execute a course of action for achieving your vision. That doesn't mean you develop the plan all by yourself. Nor does it mean you sketch out the barest details of a plan and then leave your followers to their own devices. Leading means balancing your involvement in the details of execution with your followers' need for independence and involvement in deciding how things get done. To lead, you must have a plan in mind; but you must also be willing to listen, learn, and experiment with alternatives suggested by your followers.

Do you set a good example?

Leaders set an example by the way they behave. Most effective leaders exhibit the following six behaviors:

1. *They are positive.* They have faith in their vision. They are excited, enthusiastic, and confident that their dreams can be accomplished. Achieving a vision isn't easy. Few people experience instant success; most meet a string of failures along the way. A good leader remains optimistic.
2. *They are committed to excellence and continuous improvement.* "We're great," they say, "but we'll get better!" Leaders know the success of even the grandest vision ultimately depends upon thousands of small, seemingly insignificant things being done extremely well.
3. *They tolerate failure.* In spite of their insistence on excellence, leaders realize not everything goes right. They know how to learn from failure, see past it, and know their followers do the same.
4. *They believe passionately in teamwork.* Leaders know little is ever accomplished by individuals on their own, but much can be accomplished by people who pool their resources and talents. Leaders discourage rivalry, interpersonal conflict, and competition between groups. Most important, leaders operate as part of the team.
5. *They are honest with themselves and others.* Trust is the foundation of leadership. Leaders know that once they lose the trust of their followers, they lose the ability to lead.
6. *They are fair in dealings with employees.* A critical role of the leader is resolving the conflicts that inevitably develop within any group. The leader will gain the trust and respect of employees only if his or her decisions are fair, reasonable, and made in the best interest of the entire group.

Anyone with an idea and enough money can start a business. But, not everyone can lead a business. Are you leading, following, or getting in the way?

7

How Your Beliefs About People Can Make or Break Your Business

While it may come as a surprise, the assumptions you hold about people in general—their attitudes, beliefs, and behavior with respect to work—strongly affect the kind of work environment you create for your business. They can also make or break your business. Consider the following two statements. Which best represents the beliefs you hold about most people most of the time?

Statement 1: People, by their very nature, dislike work and will avoid it when possible. They have little ambition, tend to shun responsibility, and like to be directed. Above all else, they want security. In order to get people to work, it is necessary to use coercion, control, and threats of punishment.

Statement 2: Work is as natural to people as resting or playing. External control and threats of punishment are not the only—or even the best—ways to get people to work. If given the chance, most people are capable of being self-directed and self-controlling. The average human being learns not only to accept, but to seek responsibility, if given the chance and offered the right rewards for achievement. The capacity to exercise a relatively high degree of imagination, ingenuity, and creativity in solving problems is widely distributed throughout the population.

The chances are you don't fully subscribe to either of these statements, but you probably lean more toward one than the other. Throughout our work lives, we are constantly interacting with our fellow workers. From these interactions, each of us begins to form—perhaps unconsciously—a set of fundamental beliefs about people in general. Consciously or unconsciously, the beliefs we form affect our behavior toward others, particularly people we employ and supervise. Your basic beliefs influence your behavior and the kind of working environment you will create for your business.

If your assumptions about people are closer to Statement 1 than to Statement 2, the chances are you will create a work environment with many controls. You will pay a great deal of attention to whether your people show up to work on time. You will establish rules, regulations, policies, and procedures for everything, or most things, you ask your employees to do, and you will be watchful to see that the rules are followed. Regardless of the type of work you need performed, you will try to break it down into simple steps. In fact, you will probably divide responsibility for "doing" and "checking." You will organize so that one person does the work and another—perhaps you—checks to see that the work was done correctly. If you are a Statement 1 type, you may have difficulty in delegating tasks or responsibilities to people, particularly if the job or assignment is very important. Perhaps unconsciously, you will be stingy with rewards and quick to punish or correct one of your people when he or she makes a mistake. To attract good employees you will try to offer slightly higher base pay or hourly wages than your competitors and stress the potential for promotion or job security as an inducement to those employees you want to attract and retain. Since you will be concerned that your best people might leave should their job security be threatened, you will be reluctant to share much information about your company's performance with employees, particularly if you are experiencing a downturn in the business. Finally, as your business grows you will create layers of managers, supervisors, and quality checkers. For every three to five workers, you will have someone you trust to oversee their work.

If the assumptions you hold about people are closer to Statement

2 than to Statement 1, your approach to managing people and the way you organize and conduct your business will be quite different. As a Statement 2-type manager, you will create a work environment that is much more open and flexible. The rules, regulations, policies, and procedures that you develop for your business will be simple and few in number. You will care much less about how the work gets performed. You are likely to be most comfortable with just giving general direction to your people and then letting them do things their own way. Instead of breaking jobs down into small steps, you will tend to assign people a "whole job" to accomplish. You will have few inspectors and supervisors, since you will expect everyone to check their own work. If you are a Statement 2 type, you may have just the opposite problem from your Statement 1 counterpart. Where he or she is reluctant to delegate tasks and responsibilities, you may have a tendency to overdelegate. While on the surface your operation may seem chaotic, that doesn't mean you aren't a tough taskmaster. The difference between you and your Statement 1 counterpart is that you pay attention almost strictly to results, where he or she is concerned not only with what was accomplished but how it was accomplished. You can be very tough when desired results aren't achieved, but you prefer to praise people rather than punish or criticize them. In respect to pay practices, you are likely to place more faith in incentives than base pay. You like to reward people for results with bonuses, but you don't think people work just for money. You therefore use a lot of token awards—caps, pins, plaques, dinners, and so on—as a way of recognizing and reinforcing your people. Most important, you spend a lot of time talking to your people about the business and the "grand mission" you have in mind. You want them to feel as excited about the business as you do. Compared to your Statement 1 counterpart you are much more open about sharing information about sales, the competition, and even your company's profits. Finally, as your business grows, you are reluctant to add managers or supervisors. Part of you resists because you don't want to become too remote from your people. Another part of you just resists creating any bureaucracy.

If you have taken any courses on management or motivation in the last thirty years, you probably have already noticed that Statements 1 and 2 are modified versions of the classic Theory X and Theory Y competing assumptions about worker motivation. They were originally suggested by Douglas McGregor in his book, *The Human Side of Enterprise,* back in 1960. McGregor argued that the Statement 1/Theory X assumptions were dead wrong, although they were the dominant assumptions of managers at the time and remain the assumptions of many managers and business owners today. McGregor proposed that business managers would benefit greatly from adopting Statement 2/Theory Y beliefs, since such beliefs would lead to a better place to work and greater productivity.

Since McGregor published his ideas, they have sparked a lot of debate and research. Numerous researchers throughout the 1960s and 1970s in particular tried to establish once and for all which set of assumptions—Statement 1/Theory X or Statement 2/Theory Y—was best. Which set of assumptions, they asked, was most correct about the majority of people and which would lead to the best and most productive work environment? After over thirty years, you would think we would have an answer. We don't. The fact is that there is no clear evidence that people in general are naturally more like the description in Statement 1 than the description in Statement 2. Does that mean that the assumptions you hold about people don't matter? Not at all. In fact, there is strong evidence to suggest that if you organize and manage your business according to Statement 1/Theory X assumptions, you just might break your business.

Here a five good reasons for operating your business according to Statement 2/Theory Y assumptions:

1. Statement 1/Theory X work doesn't exist anymore. We can no longer break down work into simple tasks as we once could. If anything, the world of business is becoming more chaotic. Out of that chaos comes complexity. Plus, it is becoming almost impossible to run a business today without taking advantage of new technology. When we introduce that technology, the manual, repetitive, simple work goes away. We are left with the complex, changing, and creative work the technology can't handle.

2. The volatility and chaos of American business today is making it increasingly difficult for any company—large or small—to offer employees a guarantee of job security. Even large corporations have been forced into massive layoffs. Chances are most of your employees have been touched in some way by corporate America's rash of layoffs and downsizing. If they don't have a relative or friend who lost a job and promise of lifelong security, they certainly have read enough about those who have. If all you have to offer your workers is the promise of a career with your company, they probably won't believe you. Today, you have to offer your employees something more than a job.

3. Statement 1/Theory X assumptions that work is primarily an economic exchange aren't valid anymore. If your people are working for you only for the money, they won't give their best effort. They will work just at the level to avoid losing their paycheck. That's just not sufficient today. If you are going to run a successful business today, you are going to have to ask for and obtain extraordinary performance from all of your people all of the time. Competition is such that it is really that tough to be successful.

4. It is clear in the 1990s that the keys to success for any company are rapid innovation, world-class quality, and superior customer service. To stay ahead today, you are going to have to be constantly finding new products, new services, and new ways of doing things to stay ahead of your competitors. In short, you are going to have to be creative and innovative. What's more, the quality of the products and services you provide had better be first class, or at least demonstrate real value to your customers. Consumers today are becoming very sophisticated and very cautious about their spending. Finally, consumers are becoming very vocal about service—or lack of service. Your customers today really want it all for their available dollars. And you had better be prepared to give it to them. But lazy, uncommitted Statement 1/Theory X employees won't produce the quality, service, and innovation your company needs to survive. Only Statement 2/Theory Y employees will do that.

5. Finally, you can no longer rely upon control and close supervision to get your people to perform. You can't be everywhere all the time. You can't watch and check everything your people do. And, you can't keep hiring checkers and watchers. One of the reasons large companies have downsized by laying off thousands of middle managers, supervisors, and inspectors is that checking and inspecting are too expensive.

At the beginning of this chapter, we presented two statements—two sets of assumptions you might hold about your people. Go back and reread Statement 2. Then, read the implications of that statement presented elsewhere in this article. If you are not managing your business according to Statement 2, reconsider what you are doing. Ask yourself what changes you need to make. More important, ask your employees how you need to change. You will be glad you did. You can't afford to operate from the wrong set of assumptions—not in today's business climate.

_8_

How to Motivate Your Employees

You hire and train employees to work for you. But you are all too often disappointed with the results. You select the best available people (even follow our advice on hiring—see Chapter 2) and you give them the best training (again you even follow our advice— see Chapter 4). Yet the people who work for you don't seem to care as much—aren't committed as much—to the success of your business as you are. Can they ever really care about the success of the business the way you do? Why can't they invest as much energy in serving your customers as they do in making personal phone calls on the job—while your customers wait? Why can't they do the job right the first time without you having to be there to watch everything they do? Why can't they just come to work on time? Why is it that they just don't seem to give a damn about how the job gets done or even if it does get done?

Unfortunately, your encounters with uncaring and uncommitted employees are not unusual. Practically every manager in every type of business, large and small, has faced the same frustrations you have faced in motivating people. Fortunately, the problem is so common that a lot of research has been conducted on why it occurs and, more important, what you as a manager can do about it. In summary, what we now know is that motivating people is as simple—and as complicated—as knowing and applying the ABCs. The ABCs that are the secret to motivating employees are not the ABCs of school. They are the ABCs of psychology.

"A" stands for Antecedent—what gets behavior started.

"B" stands for Behavior—what people say or do.

"C" stands for Consequences—what happens to people as a result of what they say or do.

The ABC model for understanding employee motivation is based upon the well-established principle of psychology that behavior (what people say or do) is strongly influenced by the consequences of that behavior (what happens to them as a result of the behavior). An antecedent (prompt, request, suggestion, demand, order, etc.) is necessary to get behavior started (to get people to do what you want them to do), but it is not enough to keep the behavior going (to keep them doing what you want them to do). If you want to keep people motivated, you have to provide consequences.

When your employees aren't doing what you want them to do, a place to start is to check and see how recently you have provided an antecedent. John is making too many personal phone calls on company time. Have you explained the company policy about personal phone calls to John? Mary has been coming late to work. Have you mentioned her tardiness and made your expectations clear to her? Explaining company policy, pointing out expectations, making sure that employees understand the rules of behavior—all of these are antecedents. They will help you get the right behavior started. They will help you "motivate" your people.

As surprising as it might be, employees may appear to be unmotivated when the problem really is that they don't know the correct behavior. No one has told them what is expected, or it has been so long since they were reminded that expectations have become fuzzy. A situation with one of our clients illustrates this type of motivation problem. Employees performed manual labor at this location where their hands, arms, and faces would become coated with grease and grime during the course of the workday. Company policy allowed employees to quit work fifteen minutes early each day to clean up before departing for home. Over a period of time, the fifteen minute early quitting had stretched to thirty minutes for many employees and to as much as forty-five minutes for some. Individual employees were repeatedly berated by their supervisors for "sneaking off" early, to no avail. Eventually, all employees were brought together in a group meeting where the written company policy was read and distributed. Employees responded that "they had never seen a written policy" and that, anyway, they understood that the unwritten policy was "you could take time at the end of the day to clean up and everybody always took a half hour or so." The immediate result of this meeting was that employees returned to taking only the approved fifteen minutes. The antecedent worked—at least initially.

Antecedents do work to get behavior started (or restarted as in the quitting-time example). The problem with antecedents is that they don't work over the long haul. It is the old story of "I tell them and tell them, but it doesn't do any good." That's where consequences come into play—the "C" part of the ABC motivation model.

Consequences—particularly positive consequences—sustain behavior over the long term. The effective use of positive consequences is the real secret to creating and maintaining a motivated work force. Also, using consequences is a much more effective and efficient means of motivating work behavior. Using antecedents is like using a starter to get a motor running. But you wouldn't want to have to depend upon the starter to keep the motor running. You would soon wear out the starter. Rather, you want the motor to keep running by itself as long as you give it enough fuel. Providing consequences to your employees is like providing fuel to a motor—your employees (once started) will run fine on their own as long as you are supplying the "fuel" they need.

Consequences (the "fuel" of motivation) come in two varieties—positive and negative. Positive consequences are the "good" things that happen to people as a result of their work behavior—the rewards and recognition for good performance. Negative consequences are the "bad" things that happen—the punishment for poor performance. Volumes of research have shown that the provision of positive consequences is the most effective means of creating a motivated work force. In fact, there is clear evidence to indicate that it is almost impossible to create a motivated work force through the use of negative consequences (punishment) alone. Yet negative consequences (punishment or the threat of punishment) are most often used to correct problem behavior or try to motivate employees to exhibit the right behavior. Since punishment is so commonly used and so frequently fails to get us what we want, we will spend a moment discussing the problems with using punishment before turning to the more effective technique—rewards and reinforcement.

Why Punishment—"Do It or Else . . ." —Doesn't Work

Punishment doesn't work—not well and not for long. It isn't that punishment can't work. It can. People will change their behavior if you can punish them in the right way. The problem with punishment is that you cannot punish people in a way that will get them to change their behavior for any length of time in a business setting. In fact, you cannot punish people and get them to really change their behavior in any setting. You can't use punishment to change the behavior of your spouse, your kids, your friends, your acquaintances, or anyone.

Punishment won't work for you because you can never punish in a way that meets the requirements for the effective use of punishment that psychologists have defined—immediacy, severity, and consistency. The classic hot stove example of effective punishment illustrates this point. If you place your hand on a hot stove, you are punished (it burns) immediately. The punishment is harsh—it really hurts—so you pull your hand away. A hot stove is consistent. It will always burn you, not just sometimes. And the stove doesn't care whose hand gets burned. The stove will burn you, your boss, your spouse, your child—it is completely fair and consistent. Place a hand on a hot stove and you get burned—period. Now think about the punishment you can hand out. Chances are it can't be immediate, it's not really that severe, and it is extremely hard to guarantee that you are always consistent. When someone does something wrong, chances are you won't know about it the minute it occurs. You find out when the customer complains maybe hours, days, or weeks later. And how severe can you really be? You can't physically hurt anyone—at least we hope not. You can yell at them.

But after a while—as we all know—people quit listening, and yelling just doesn't do any good. The most severe thing you can do is fire people. But if you are like most of us, firing somebody is not something you particularly enjoy doing. Anyway, you can't fire everybody. Finally, there is the matter of consistency. You try to be consistent. But the fact is you can't watch people all the time. Somewhere, sometime, somebody is going to do exactly the same behavior and go unpunished. You won't see it happen—you won't catch them in the act—and you'll have a hard time justifying punishing them if you didn't catch them doing it. Any punishment you can hand out is weak because it just won't pass the "immediate, severe, consistent" test. But let's say you do try to punish people when they do something wrong. What happens?

Something called the "punishment effect" has been well established in research. Essentially, it says: "When punishment is used to control behavior, people perform at a level just sufficient to avoid the punishment." Speed limits are a good example of the "punishment effect." Not too long ago, the speed limit on most major American roads was 55 miles per hour. When that was true, we used to ask people all over the country how fast they usually drove in a 55-mile-per-hour speed-limit zone. Consistently, they told us that they drove between 63 and 65 miles per hour. A few said they drove a little faster. When we asked why they all drove 63 or 65 when the speed limit was 55, they said: "If you drive faster than 65, you'll get a ticket." Practically everyone we spoke with had a certain speed—above the speed limit—they felt they could drive without getting a ticket—without getting punished. Everyone drove at a speed just short of the point at which they thought they might be punished.

Another story that illustrates the punishment effect and the futility of trying to force performance goes like this:

Years ago, a farmer was going to market in his cart loaded with vegetables. Having started out late, the farmer was in a hurry for fear of missing the market opening. Halfway to the market, his mule stopped dead still in the middle of the road and refused to move. No amount of cracking the whip or flapping the reins would get the mule started again. Finally, in anger, the farmer jumped down from the cart and began to beat the mule with a stick. Still the mule refused to move. The farmer became incensed, rushed to the side of the road, and gathered up all of the sticks, twigs, and dry bushes he could find. He piled it under the mule and set it on fire. The mule moved—just far enough to pull the cart squarely over the fire.

The farmer punished the mule and the mule responded—just enough to avoid the punishment.

The same punishment effect occurs in the work setting. Inevitably when we go into a business where managers try to control behavior through discipline or punishment, we find the same phenomenon. Employees soon learn the minimum performance sufficient to avoid the discipline or punishment. Everybody performs fairly close to that level. The tragedy is that that level is usually far below the level of performance that is possible. Because of the punishment effect, these managers get minimum performance from their people.

Why Positive Consequences— "Do It and You Get . . ."—Do Work

If punishment doesn't work, your only other choice is reinforcement. If you can't force people to perform, you have to entice them. Repeatedly, reinforcement (providing something that people want after the occurrence of desired behavior) has been demonstrated to be the most effective method for attaining long-term maximum performance.

Thinking of different ways to say "thank you" can be the hardest part of the task for entrepreneurs. However, there are several different reinforcers you can use to make your praise known.

Social Reinforcers

Social reinforcers are the easiest, and often the most effective, way to say "thank you." One of the best is a simple, verbal "thank you." Employees often tell us that in recognition of a good job, they'd like nothing more than to hear those words.

Other social reinforcers include a nod, smile, or pat on the back. And although you shouldn't ask for additional behavior when saying thanks, offering an employee a *choice* of job-related activities can be an effective reinforcer. Increased job responsibilities, a choice of job assignments, or opportunities for extra training are all options that can strengthen desired behavior.

Tangible Reinforcers

Tangible reinforcers are monetary or material items given in appreciation of good performance. Awards such as Employee of the Month are the most popular tangible reinforcers, but they are often misused. Too often, these types of awards become insulting to employees because they are given to those who don't actually meet the performance levels represented by the award.

To make tangible reinforcers work, follow two simple guidelines. First, make sure the award is given on the basis of meeting specific criteria. For example, "sales per month," "defects per unit of product," "customer satisfaction rating"—anyone reaching a certain preestablished goal on such measures wins. Second, make sure there are no arbitrary restrictions on how many people can win the award or how many times a single person can win.

An important thing to remember about tangible reinforcers is that to be effective, they need to be coupled with social reinforcers. In our consulting, we've talked to many people who question the sincerity of a pen set or button because no verbal praise came with it. Give the reward, but don't forget the heartfelt thanks.

Reinforcing Memos

Reinforcing memos are more formal than social or tangible reinforcers and should be used to reward important behaviors. They are appropriate in several situations. One is when a business owner has very little face-to-face contact with the employee, as in a sales department where salespeople are often away from the office. Another is when the behavior is crucial or if the employee has demonstrated exceptional effort, such as trying to meet sudden deadlines or coping with major changes. Reinforcing memos add variety to verbal reinforcement. While a verbal "thank you" is the most effective way to reward people, everyone gets tired of the same thing all the time. Memos also supply a permanent record of good performance.

Making Your Reinforcement Count

Regardless of whether you use social reinforcers, tokens, or reinforcing memos, there are several guidelines you should follow to make your "thank you" really count:

Be specific.

Everyone engages in hundreds of behaviors each day. Consequently, if you want to thank employees for a job well done, you must be very specific about what you are thanking them for doing. A vague "Good job" or "I appreciate that" just won't do. If you are not specific about what the employee did, he or she may misinterpret the praise, and you will lose the opportunity to shape desirable behavior. For example, instead of saying, "Hey, John, thanks for the help yesterday," say, "John, I really appreciate the fact that you volunteered to stay late last night and help with loading the delivery van even though it wasn't your job."

Thank people immediately.

Lack of immediacy diminishes the impact of a "thank you." So many times you see or hear an employee do something good, but then you get distracted and don't remember to praise the person until hours, days, or weeks later. By then, of course, the immediacy of the reinforcement is lost. Not only will the "thank you" be less effective than it could have been, but the employee might even take it as an insult. "If she really thought I did a good job," the employee may think, "why did she take so long to get around to saying so?" Being late with a "thank you" is like being late with a birthday present. No matter how nice the present is, it loses something when it's late.

Make "thank you" contingent on performance.

It's nice to say "thank you," but you shouldn't say "thank you" just to be nice. You should say it to show your employees that you appreciate good performance and that you want them to repeat that behavior. If you hand out "thank yous" without linking them to performance, they lose their power to encourage good performance.

Remember this when you hand out turkeys to all your employees at Thanksgiving or give everyone a Christmas bonus (regardless of how well they performed during the year). Rewards that aren't directly tied to performance won't encourage better performance. If you want your employees to work harder, your "thank you" must be contingent on performance. Perform and you get a reward; don't perform and you don't get it. It's that simple.

Make your "thank you" proportional to what was done.

Often, the simple words "thank you" or "I really appreciate that" are enough. But there are times when something more is needed—a gift, a plaque, or a bonus perhaps. Think about what the employee did and what it meant to your company. Then make the nature of your "thank you" match the value of the performance. Don't be like the airline executive who told us, "We thank our people all the time. Whenever we have a bomb scare and an employee volunteers to look for the bomb *and finds it,* we send him or her a letter of commendation."

Individualize your "thank you."

Where, when, and how you say "thank you" must be tailored to the person you are thanking if your reinforcement is to have any power. Some people like public praise; some prefer to be praised in private. Fifty-yard-line seats at a big football game would be the perfect "thank you" for some employees; others would prefer tickets to the ballet. Saying "thank you" is like buying a present for someone—you need to know something about the person in order to choose the right gift. The more you know about your employees, the easier it will be for you to say "thank you" in a way that really matters to them.

You must get to know your employees if you hope to find the right reinforcements to motivate them. You've probably heard the suggestion, "Manage by walking around." That's good advice. Get out of your office and get to know your staff. Listen to what they talk about. Watch what they do during breaks or on their lunch hour. Ask about their plans after work or on holidays. If you spend enough time around your employees, you will learn a lot about how to motivate them.

Personalize your "thank you."

In order to really matter, your "thank you" has to be personal. The reward or recognition that you offer shouldn't come from the corporation; it should come directly from you. When you thank people, tell them what their good performance means to you personally. Tell them how much *you* appreciate what they did. For example, if you want to thank someone in writing, don't send a typed form letter. Instead, send a short, handwritten note. And instead of writing, "XYZ Corp. would like to express its appreciation to you for . . ." write, "Dear John, I wanted to take a moment to write to you personally and tell you how much I appreciate . . ."

Be sincere.

Don't thank someone for a job well done unless you really mean it. Saying "thank you" is not something you can fake. If you don't feel it, don't do it. Employees can see through insincerity every time, and one instance of praise that's less than heartfelt will render all your subsequent "thank yous" suspect.

Be consistent.

Don't just thank some of the people some of the time. You'll be accused of playing favorites. Reinforcement will work only if you do it consistently. There are two secrets to consistency. First, think through the results you want and the behavior that gets those results, and discuss it with your people. For example, you and your staff need to agree not only that customer service is important, but also how customer service is measured and what behaviors lead to good customer service.

Second, make reinforcement a regular part of meetings with your employees. This not only ensures consistent reinforcement, since it's done on a regular basis, but it also makes your staff meetings more positive. Too often, meetings are devoted to nothing but a discussion of problems. Building reinforcement into the regular agenda ensures that at least part of each meeting is spent celebrating successes.

Vary your reinforcement.

Would you want to receive the same present every year on your birthday? Of course not. It's the same with "thank yous." If you want to make your "thank you" matter, you have to vary where, when, and how you reinforce people. One month, celebrate completing a major project with balloons and champagne; after the next big project, try giving everybody who contributed a small trophy.

It's not so much *what* you do; it's the mystery that matters. Again, think of your "thank you" as a present. A present is more fun to open when you have no idea what it is. Of course, your employees should feel confident that their hard work will be appreciated, but it's good to keep them guessing about just what you might do to say "thank you."

Never mix reinforcement with punishment
or ask for additional behavior.

"But" is the worst word you can use when reinforcing people. It makes people suspicious—they start waiting for the other shoe to drop. If your work environment has not been very positive in the past, people will probably be a little hesitant to accept your thanks at first. When you praise them, they may think, "I wonder what he wants?" or "What is she setting me up for now?"

You dilute the impact of praise when you immediately follow it with criticism or a request for something more. Don't say, "John, I really appreciate the overtime you worked last night to help us with the inventory. Now, could you stay tonight to help Bill with the job he has to do?" Simply thank him for his help.

Of course, this doesn't mean you can't correct problem behavior. Just make sure you don't discuss problems at the same time you are praising a person. Let some time pass so that the two concerns will be seen as separate.

If you follow these ten guidelines, you will be able to say "thank you" in a way that will motivate your employees to higher and higher levels of performance.

A Word About Awards and Contests

A popular method of reinforcing good performance that many companies have adopted is a contest or Employee of the Month award. Unfortunately, many of these programs have little, if any, impact on performance. For example, in a recent American Productivity Center survey, only about a third of the companies surveyed rated such recognition programs as being very effective. Why? Simply because many of these programs violate the guidelines for effective reinforcement we just listed. For example, many such awards are based upon subjective criteria. Even employees who win the awards don't know exactly why they won. As a result, the awards become noncontingent. Employees cannot see a direct connection between their behavior and the award. Additionally, many of these programs are designed so that only a few employees can win the award. For example, no matter how well employees perform, there can be only one Employee of the Month. A lot of employees don't try for the award because the odds are against them winning. We are not saying that you should not establish some type of employee award. What we are saying is that you should make sure it conforms to the guidelines for reinforcement. For example, instead of an Employee of the Month award, why not establish a "club" people can become part of once they achieve a certain level of performance? One of our clients has a very effective recognition program they call the President's Club. All employees who reach a certain level of measured performance get a banner, pin, or certificate signifying that they have earned membership in the President's Club. To retain membership, they have to continue to perform at a certain minimum level. All employees have a chance to earn membership, and they do so based upon purely objective criteria.

What About Money?

Does money motivate? There is a tremendous amount of debate over the answer to this question. On one side, we agree with those who argue that you can't buy performance. We agree that paying people more is not the answer. There are a lot of highly paid people who don't perform very well, as we all know. On the other hand, there is a lot of evidence that people will work harder and smarter if given the opportunity to earn incentive pay.

Does money motivate? We think it can if an incentive program is designed and implemented in the right way. For example:

1. People will perform at higher levels if given the opportunity to earn variable incentive compensation. However, the incentive pay must be separate and distinct from base salary. You should even pay the incentive on a separate check. Your people should understand that the incentive is something they earn for objectively measured improvements in performance. It is not guaranteed like base pay.
2. To really motivate people, the potential must exist for in-

centive pay that is equal to 10 percent or more of base pay. For many employees, a 1 or 2 percent bonus just isn't enough to entice them to perform at higher levels.

3. The criteria for earning incentive pay should be performance above a base level on an reliable, objective measure that is clearly and unmistakably related to what employees do. They must see the connection between what they do and the incentive pay they earn. And subjectivity must be removed. If they perform, they have to feel certain that they will earn the incentive bonus. Relatedly, if you want to drive performance, the measure you use to calculate whether a bonus was earned must be a true measure of employee performance. For example, if employees have little control over profits—because pricing decisions and market conditions have a great effect—then a profit-based formula for calculating bonuses won't work.

Motivating employees for maximum performance isn't easy. It will take a lot of your time and effort. But it is easier than correcting the problems caused by unmotivated people. And it is more efficient and cost effective than constantly hiring additional people to make up for the halfhearted efforts of those employees you currently have. With some thought and effort in applying the motivation techniques we described in this chapter, there is no reason why you should not get significant improvements in performance— 20 percent, 50 percent, or even 100 percent better.

_9_

Building a Winning Team

Whether on the playing field or in business, teams win—individuals don't. People working together make it happen. Building a winning team is critical for success, whether your goal is scoring touchdowns or winning customers. But your employees—your players—don't come to you as members of a team. How, then, do you mold a group of individuals into a winning team?

A "winning team" is more than the sum of its members. It is more than just a collection of individuals. Winning teams have six basic characteristics in common:

1. Players focus on a common purpose. In sports, the purpose is to win the game. In spite of their individual differences, players on a winning team are bound together by this common sense of "who we are" and "what we are here to do." Team members are able to make personal sacrifices for the good of the team because they share this common goal.

2. In addition to the larger purpose, players share smaller, specific goals—making touchdowns, gaining yardage, and so on. Winning teams recognize, as the great coach Bear Bryant once said, that to win the game they have to get all the "itty bitty, teeny weeny things right."

3. Winning teams keep score. And they keep track of the little things, not just the big things. A winning team not only knows the final score, it also knows how it scored on yards rushing, yards passing, and time of possession. Winning teams rec-

ognize that performance on those "little things" must be monitored and improved if they are to keep winning.

4. Winning teams share the rewards of success. The cheers of the crowd aren't just for a chosen few; they are for every player who made it happen. The surest way to become a losing team is to let a few superstars hog the applause. On a winning team, even the superstars know that they didn't win alone, and they are generous with their praise for all the others who made the difference between success and failure.

5. Every player knows his or her role and how to play that role to perfection. Sure, all winning teams recruit "natural talent." But they know that natural talent is rarely enough—it has to be molded and shaped through training, conditioning, practice, planning, and careful preparation. And the training never stops. Winning teams recognize that even the best natural talent can always get better.

6. Every player is expected to be involved in winning all the time. Sure, every player on the team can't be physically involved in every play, but all players are expected to be mentally and emotionally involved in every play. Winning teams don't have players who simply warm the bench.

Creating a Winning Environment

You must create an environment where your employees—your players—can develop the characteristics of a winning team. Here are some suggestions.

Step One: Clearly Define the Mission of Your Business

What is the mission of your business? If you think it is to make money, you're wrong. Sure, every business needs to make money, but you're not in business just to make money. If you think you are, you will never build a winning team. In fact, you won't even stay in business very long. Years ago, Peter Drucker, the noted management writer, observed that the mission of every business should be to find and keep customers. "A business is not defined by the company's name, statutes or articles of incorporation," said Drucker. "It is defined by the want the customer satisfies when he buys a product or service. To satisfy the customer is the mission and purpose of every business."

Your first task in building a winning team is to clearly define the mission of your business. To do that, ask yourself the following questions:

- Who are (or should be) our customers?
- What need do those customers seek to satisfy when doing business with us?
- How do those customers evaluate our success in meeting that need?

Simple questions, right? But once you try to answer them, you will find they are tough questions. Even top executives in the largest and most successful businesses struggle to answer them. Yet every successful business is successful precisely because someone found an answer to these questions.

Start by simply writing down the questions and your first response. Then revise your response until you are satisfied. Once you have your initial answers, check them out with your spouse, friends, and business associates. Ask your employees what they think. Most important, ask your customers. Pick a few of your current customers and ask them: "How can we serve you better?" "What do you like (or dislike) about doing business with us?" You may be surprised at the answers.

Step Two: Make Sure Every Employee Understands the Mission

Once you have a clear definition of your business's mission, you have to communicate it to your employees. But effective communication is rarely easy. There are many ways that people can misunderstand or misinterpret your message. Here are some things you can do to get your message across.

1. Prepare a written statement of your business mission and distribute it to your employees. Try to limit your statement to a few carefully worded sentences—or, at most, a paragraph or two. Your challenge here is to write a short statement that incorporates everything you have learned about your customers, their needs, and what your business must do to satisfy their needs. There is no shortcut to writing this document. You just write it, revise it, and revise it again. But take your time. It has to be perfect, or at least as close to perfect as you can get.

2. Develop a motto and post it everywhere. Ford's motto is: "Quality Is Job One." What's "Job One" in your business? What are the few words that symbolize all you are trying to say in the statement of your business mission? One of the best mottos we have seen was used by one of our clients in the direct mail business. Their motto was just two words— "Service First." But those two words spoke volumes. Signs were posted everywhere, plaques were on desks, and employees even wore T-shirts—all emblazoned with the words "Service First" as a constant reminder.

3. Live the mission. Written and spoken words are one way to communicate your mission, but your actions are much more important than your words. The surest way to make employees understand your mission is to live it. How do you spend your time? How do you treat customers? If you laugh at a joke about a "stupid" customer, you send one message. If you drop what you are doing to respond immediately to a customer's "stupid" and "unreasonable" request, you send a completely different message. Pay attention not just to what you tell your employees, but to how you behave. Does your behavior match your words?

Step Three: Develop Specific Goals

Communicating your business mission is one thing; knowing how you intend to achieve your mission is another. If you are going to build a winning team, you and your employees must know exactly what it takes to win. What are the critical levels of performance that will lead to success in your business? Most businesses compete in just a few areas, such as the quality of the product or service they provide, their ability to deliver a product or service within a specified time, or service at a certain cost.

You should identify five to ten measurable areas of performance that are critical for achieving your business mission. To identify these areas, do the following:

1. Review your mission statement. Your mission was derived from what you learned about the needs and wants of your customers. Now break these needs and wants down into specific, measurable areas of performance. For example, if "quality" was a critical customer concern, think about how you can measure the quality of your product or service.

2. Make a list of your competitors or potential competitors. Regardless of your business, you have competition or the potential for competition. Sure, right now you might be lucky enough to be the only provider of a particular product or service for miles around. But never assume that your "monopoly" will stay that way for long, particularly if your success is due to customer demand. Before long, someone else will recognize that customer demand, and you will find a new competitor just across the street. Before you can set goals, you must have your competition clearly in mind.

3. Set long-term goals to beat your competition. With your competitors firmly in mind, decide on the level of performance you need in each of your critical areas in order to beat the competition. You can find out how well your competition is doing by asking around or simply observing them. If you belong to a national business association, check with it to see if it compiles any statistics concerning industry standards in the key areas you have identified. If you don't have any competition right now, or if you have no reliable source for competitive information, you may just have to guess. Regardless, decide upon a level of performance you think you'll need to be the best in your field.

Then comes the crucial step. Consult with your employees and let them help you set a performance goal or target for each area.

% ON TIME DELIVERY

Don't just set the goals yourself in isolation. Share with your employees what you have learned about the performance level you need in order to compete, and ask them what they think they can do to help reach these goals. If the long-term goal you have set seems too difficult, try setting an interim target or short-term goal they can shoot for right away.

Step Four: Develop and Implement a Scorekeeping System

Once you have specific and measurable goals, the next step in creating a winning team is to develop and implement a system for keeping score. You need a "scoreboard"—a highly visible, easily understood way of conveying how well your team is performing versus how well it should be performing.

Find a location your employees visit frequently—such as a lunchroom or locker room—and devote part of the wall space to a large, colorful scoreboard. Post graphs like the one shown detailing each of the five or ten critical areas of performance you are tracking.

Once you have the graphs posted, hold a meeting with your employees to go over the graphs. Explain each measure being graphed and why it is important. Show the ultimate goal and discuss how you arrived at the goal. Finally—and most important—discuss with your employees how their behavior can affect performance.

Step Five: Make Performance Matter by Sharing the Rewards

Feedback and positive reinforcement are crucial for building a winning team. Your scoreboard takes care of feedback. Now you must use reinforcement to make employees care about their performance. Praise employees, give them recognition for improved performance, and reward progress toward goals in a meaningful way. Consider offering awards such as caps, buttons, plaques, or certificates for improved performance or for achieving goals. Try to tie these gifts to your motto. For example, if your motto is "Service First," you could start a "Service First Club" where everyone who achieves a certain level of performance can win a cap, button, or coffee cup with "Service First" printed on it. Make sure everyone has a fair opportunity to win the award, and follow the rules for reinforcing employees' behavior we discussed in Chapter 8. Eventually, you should consider tying employees' compensation to their performance in the areas you are tracking, as we suggested in Chapter 5.

Step Six: Make Sure Employees Understand Their Roles and Have a Chance to Become Involved in Improving Performance

Your employees' success in reaching their performance goals depends upon two things. First, they must understand the goals and how their behavior contributes to attaining them. Second, they must have a way to become involved in deciding how to change their behavior to achieve the goals.

The best way to achieve both of these is to meet with your employees on a regular basis (once a month or once a week) to discuss performance. In these meetings, be sure to

- Reinforce good or improved performance by pointing out things individuals (or the group) did that contributed to an improvement in performance.
- Review current performance in the areas you are tracking.

Bring your graphs to the meeting and point out any changes in performance.

- Brainstorm with your employees to get ideas for improving performance through changes in employee behavior.
- Conclude the meeting by agreeing on specific action that will be taken to improve performance, and assign individual employees responsibility for implementing these changes. At subsequent meetings, follow up on these plans by asking these employees to report on what was done.

Following these basic guidelines will help you turn your employees into a winning team.

_10_

The Importance of Involving Employees

Why should you have to involve your employees in running your business? After all, it is your business. You've worked hard to reach the position where you make the decisions. You've taken the risk in starting your own business. They haven't. You left a secure job working for somebody else because you wanted to be your own boss. You didn't want to have to do it their way. You wanted to do it your way. What's wrong with that? Just that if you insist on running your business "your way" and only "your way," you may destroy your business. The vast majority of small businesses fail in the first five years. Many of these businesses fail precisely because the owner/manager insisted upon running the business "his way" or "her way." These owners and managers failed to get their people involved. They tried to make all the decisions themselves. They insisted that there was only one right way to do anything—their way. They "demanded" and "ordered." They wouldn't listen to employee ideas or suggestions. Their approach was "check your mind at the door" and "just do what I tell you to do." And they did exactly what they were told to do, even if it was wrong. The order—"No refunds without a sales receipt"—was carried out precisely. What did they care if the customer without a sales receipt was *the major customer?* So what if he got mad and swore never to do business with the company again? "No sales receipt" meant "no refund." That was the rule. Period.

Ten Good Reasons for Involving Your Employees

Why involve your employees in running your business? It's very simple. You have to involve your people because it is practically impossible for your business to be successful unless your people are committed to making it successful. And they won't care if your business is successful unless you involve them in how the business is run.

Consider what almost any business needs to be successful today and how important employee involvement is in making success happen.

Quality Demands That People Be Involved

The quality of your product or service is the most important determinant of whether your business survives. There's just no doubt about that. If you don't deliver quality products and services as determined by how your customers view it, they are going to go elsewhere. If you don't believe quality is that important, just try foisting junk on your customers. They'll leave you in droves.

Now what does quality have to do with involving employees? Everything. You can't inspect or control your way to quality. Quality has to be built in, not tacked on. You have to make the product or provide the service right the first time. The only person who can do that is the employee. And he or she isn't going to do that unless he wants to. Just try making somebody want to do something. You can't. Oh, you might be able to make them do it occasionally. But you can't make them want to do it. And that's the point. Either employees want to produce a quality job or they don't. They decide what they want to do, not you. And they aren't going to want to do anything unless they are involved.

Service Demands That People Be Involved

Second to quality (a close second) in determining whether your business succeeds or fails is customer service. Even if you give 'em great quality, mess up the service and your customers will still leave. So where does service come from? It comes during those thousands of small moments when one employee interacts with one customer. It comes during all those tiny "moments of truth" when how that customer feels about your company is determined by how that employee behaves. Just as in the case of quality, you can't control your way to service. Your employee provides service or doesn't provide service, and you can't control it or make it happen. You can't be there during all of those thousands of moments to make sure it occurs. Your employee decides to provide service or not. And he won't provide service unless he has a reason to do it. If he isn't involved in the business, he won't have a reason.

Performance Demands That People Be Involved

Anyone who has ever tried to provide real quality and real customer service knows it's damn hard to do. You don't get quality and service from just average or okay performance. You get it from people trying hard to make it happen. Try forcing people to try hard. Try making people do their utmost best. You can't. Oh, you may be able to beat them into okay performance, but you're not going to beat them into super performance. People give their best because they want to give their best.

Everything Else Demands That People Be Involved

Beyond quality and service—or as an integral part of them—are innovation, creativity, flexibility, and quick response to changing customer demands. Now just try to force somebody to be innovative—or creative—or flexible—or to "get on the stick" and get something done real fast. You can't, can you? Again, you want your people to be innovative; you want them to be creative; you want them to be flexible; you want them to really be "quick about it"—well, if they want to they will. And what makes them "want to"? If they are involved, if there is something in it for them, if they are partners—then, maybe then, they'll want to. You can't beat them into it.

Responsiveness Demands That People Be Involved

Let's just take one of these things you've got to have to make it in business today—quick response to customer needs, demands, questions, concerns. If you're going to respond quickly, that means somebody has to make a quick decision. You can't wait while level after level of managers mull it over. Well, maybe you can wait, but you can be certain your customer won't wait. So who's going to have to make the decision? The employee—the person closest to the customer—is going to have to make the decision. That means your employees are going to have to be informed, empowered, and trusted to make the decisions that have to be made to keep the customer happy. And they are going to have to even be allowed to make decisions that occasionally turn out to be wrong. Now, people who are controlled, who are subordinate, and who are subservient to other people don't make decisions. They get beat up if they try. We all know that. It's the nature of the relationship. Equal partners make decisions. Equal partners have the information to make decisions. Equal partners have the authority to make decisions. And equal partners are allowed to be wrong sometimes.

Technology Demands That People Be Involved

One thing that's driving all this partnership and team stuff is technology. Whether you want it or not, you know you've got to have technology. If you don't invest in automation, you know you're going to be beat. But there are several curious things about technology. First, technology does away with the manual, repetitive jobs. It leaves behind the thinking, creative stuff. So when you put in technology, it takes away the stuff people can be made to do and leaves behind the things people have to want to do. Second, technology usually means that people have to work together to get things done. They have to do all those things like share information, cooperate, work as a team. People have to be involved in making technology work. Third, technology that is well cared for by attentive, responsible, creative, and innovative people has enormous value. But watch out if you leave the technology alone. That same processor that can do so much good can also eat up tons of raw materials, generate enormous piles of waste, destroy customer relationships, and sink your business. And it can do it so fast. All you need running the stuff is a bunch of yoyos who don't give a damn, and boy, are you in trouble. Finally, all that expensive technology is just a pile of silicone chips until people do something with it. If you don't believe you better be concerned about the people side of introducing new technology, just go talk to GM.

People Demand That They Be Involved

People demand more from their jobs today. Yes, it's true. We've all gotten a little selfish about what we want and expect from the people who employ us. A job and a paycheck just aren't enough. We all want more than that. Maybe it's because we haven't got a whole lot else. Maybe it's because of what's happened to families and churches and communities. Maybe it's because we've all been exposed to so much through global media coverage that we aren't so parochial in our interest, ideas, and beliefs anymore. I don't know what it is. But we all seem to want a whole lot. And we look to our work to give us a lot of what we want—like belonging, meaning, significance, purpose, and all those things. Now, the trick here is that the people who seem to want the most out of their jobs—who demand the most—are the people who are really in demand. They're in short supply and are going to become in even shorter supply. (Blame your educational system for a lot of that—but we won't go into education and all its problems right here.) You can be sure the people who can think, be creative, be innovative, solve problems, get results—those are exactly the people who'll tell you to "take your job and shove it" if all you've got to offer them is a job. They can do that. They don't have to have your job. Your competitor would love to have them. If you don't involve people, provide them with something more than a paycheck, if you don't listen to them, if you don't let them know you care what they think, if you don't make them partners—they're going to leave you flat. You'll be stuck with the leftovers. You know—the people who can't think, reason, solve problems; who —for God's sake—can't even read and write.

You Don't Have Much Choice

Even if you could somehow control your way to survival in the crazy, competitive business world, where are you going to get the controllers? Your employees have to be self-managing and self-controlling. Are you really going to staff up with middle manager "watchers" and "prison guards" (what we call the "burden") that don't do anything but try to beat other people into doing things? Come on now—who's kidding whom? Do that and your indirect labor costs will go out of sight and you'll tube the whole thing.

Involvement Is All That's Left for Most of Us

Now, if you're stuck with a flatter organization without those levels to promote people through, then people at the bottom don't have a whole lot of places to go. They're stuck. Try trapping people in a mindless, dead-end job with no hope of a way out and see how long they stay there. Well, you may not be able to change the dead-end part, but you better do something about the mindless part. You better put something into the jobs that are left to make them interesting or challenging. Otherwise, the folks are just going to check out mentally or physically.

It Works!

Finally, you need to involve people and build teams because—you know something?—it works. The fact is, given the chance, people are pretty amazing. It really is true that ordinary people—Tom and Joe and Jane and even old Ralph—who have sat around for years and not done a damn thing get turned on when they are given responsibility and meaning and purpose and accountability and are made to feel they matter and are worth something. They really aren't that different from you or me or anybody else. But then, why did we ever think they were?

Three Keys to Super Employee Involvement

If employee involvement is so important to the success of your business, how do you make it happen? There are really only three keys to getting super involvement from all of your people.

Share Information

The first key to involving people in running your business is to open up and share information with your employees. It's definitely *not true* that your people need to know just enough to do their jobs. Your people need to know as much as you can share about your business. They need to know your dreams about your business. What kind of business are you trying to build? What is going to make your business special and attract the kind of customers you want to attract? Who are your competitors? What are your strengths and weaknesses compared to your competitors? You need to share as much financial information as you can. What does it cost to turn on the lights? How valuable is your inventory? What does it mean to the business if you get 1 percent shrinkage instead of 2 percent? Sure, some of this information is sensitive. But if your employees don't know this information, they won't care about the success of the business. And if they don't care, they won't perform.

Ask and Listen

It is a human frailty. Most of us tend to talk more than we listen. Instead of asking our employees what they think should be done to solve a problem, reduce costs, or improve performance, we tell them what we think. All too often, our approach to employees is "just shut up and listen." Pretty soon, they do just that. They develop the attitude, "So what if what we are being told to do won't work?" They just do what they are told to do, even if it is wrong. What do we miss when we just order people to do things and don't listen to their ideas? We miss a lot of good ideas. More important, when our employees aren't involved in deciding how to do something, they aren't committed to doing it right. They just go through the motions. Compare an employee going through the motions to one who is dedicated to making his ideas work. You'll have no trouble spotting the difference.

Share the Rewards

The final key to involving employees is to share the rewards of success with your employees. If you want your people to really care about the success of your business, make sure there is something in it for them. Recognize their contributions. Let them know that they are important and that you value their ideas. And let them share in the financial success of your business. Sure, you made the investment and took the financial risk of starting your own business. It is only right that a substantial portion of the financial rewards of success go to you. But don't leave out your employees. Let them share in the profits and cost savings they help you create. They'll return your generosity tenfold in additional savings and profits.

Why involve your employees in running your business? Because employee involvement is one of the most important things you can do to ensure the survival and success of your business. When you share information with employees, ask for their ideas and suggestions, and share the financial and other rewards of success with employees, you will develop a high-performance work force. You'll have a team of people as dedicated to the success of your business as you are. How can you lose with that?

__11__

Correcting Problem Behavior

Tom is one of your best machine operators, but he insists upon running his equipment constantly and pushing it to its limits. Not once have you seen him shut the machine down to perform the cleaning and regular preventive maintenance you know is essential. Sure, you appreciate the fact that Tom is dedicated to getting production out, but you are concerned about the long term. That equipment has to be cleaned regularly and maintained if it is going to last. If Tom doesn't take care of it, pretty soon you know he's going to ruin a piece of expensive equipment. If there is one thing you can't stand, it's somebody who doesn't take proper care of his or her equipment. The more you think about it, the angrier you get.

Joan just talks too much. Every time you walk through the store, she is over talking to Betty about one thing or another. You're not paying her to talk, you're paying her to wait on customers and stock the shelves. There are plenty of things that need to be done. This excessive chatter has got to stop.

Recently, Dan has developed a really bad attitude. He seems sullen and moody all the time. Yesterday, he even snapped at a customer. This morning, when you tried to say something to him about yesterday's incident, he just slammed down the order book, said something about "not having to take that kind of thing from a customer or anybody," and stomped off.

Neal is a hard worker, but recently he has started coming in late. At first, it was just a few minutes late, but yesterday he was almost one hour late. Bob got mad because he had to stay overtime to fill in until Neal finally arrived. Neal's tardiness has got to stop.

Martha has taken emergency personal leave five times just in the last month. You know she lost her baby-sitter for her youngest child and has had problems finding a new one. Regardless, every time she is out on short notice you have to scramble to get someone to fill in for her. Something has to change. This can't continue.

These are just a few examples of the kind of problem employee behavior every manager faces eventually. And it isn't just low performers who exhibit this type of behavior. Even your best employees can have a bad day or even a series of bad days. It happens even in the best and most motivated work force. These bad days—the problem employee behavior—are not only frustrating, but if handled poorly can cost you an otherwise good employee or, worse, hurt your business.

In order to correct an employee's problem behavior, you must conduct a one-on-one counseling session. But before you call the employee into your office for a discussion, you need to do some planning.

Step One: Pinpoint the Problem

You can't begin to correct a problem until it is clearly defined. To correct problem employee behavior, at some point you are going to have to meet with the employee to discuss the problem. When you do, you will need to state the problem clearly and have the "facts" to support your contention that a problem really exists. A problem exists only when there are clear expectations for performance and actual performance fails to meet these expectations. Therefore, you need to get the facts on actual performance, facts on the standards or expectations for performance, and establish the extent to which there is a gap between the standards/expectations and actual performance. For example, you haven't seen Tom shut down his machine to perform preventive maintenance. But how do you know the maintenance has actually not been performed? Is it possible that Tom has performed the maintenance, but that you didn't see him do it? What records exist about when maintenance is performed? What are the standards or expectations about preventive maintenance? Are they documented? Neal has been coming in late. But how often? How late was he? Is there a written company policy about tardiness? Before you take action to meet with an employee to discuss a problem, make sure you have defined the problem clearly and collected all the relevant facts.

Step Two: Make Sure the Problem Is Really Worth Solving

As the saying goes, "There are problems and then there are *problems.*" No matter how irritating or frustrating you may find a particular employee's behavior, that behavior you dislike may or may not be a problem for the business. Changing an employee's behavior takes time and effort, and costs the business. Some behaviors you personally dislike may not be worth changing simply because they don't have a significant impact on the bottom line results of the business. Many managers, to their ultimate regret, have created more problems for the business than they solved by focusing on behavior quirks of employees that, while personally irritating to the manager, caused little if any problem for bottom-line performance. We have seen managers get involved in morale- and performance-destroying confrontations with good employees over such issues as hair length, dress codes, the arrangement of office furniture, and a host of other issues that, in fact, had little to do with performance. While in some jobs hair length and dress may have an impact on performance, in many occupations such matters are irrelevant. Just make sure you focus on results when deciding if a "problem" is really a "*problem.*"

Thomas Gilbert, in his book *Human Competence: Engineering Worthy Performance,* tells the following story of a budding entrepreneur who succumbed to the trap of focusing on a problem with employee behavior that turned out not to be a problem at all. The story, which Gilbert maintains is true and only slightly embellished, concerns one Barton Hogg, who had secured a military contract to salvage lead from spent bullets on a Fort Jackson firing range. Hogg anticipated extracting over $100,000 of lead by employing day laborers to sift through the sand on the firing range. He had even worked out the most efficient method for shoveling the sand into hardware-cloth boxes, sifting out the spent bullets, and dumping them into milk pails. Hogg's first group of sixty laborers worked out well. They followed his instructions to the letter and soon were working at a organized and steady pace. It was Hogg's second group of fifty college students that gave him problems. Gilbert described the scene as follows: "The truck [carrying the students] arrived annoyingly late, and the platoon poured off in shouting disarray. . . . They listened to Hogg's instructions with the same blank inattention they had learned to give their professors—and they followed his instructions just as poorly. . . . Soon the shovels were discarded, and they were scraping the sieves directly into the sand. Jokes and ribaldry poured out faster than the lead." Hogg tried shouting at the students to follow his instructions. He appealed to their sense of responsibility. He did everything he could think of to get them to follow his carefully worked out instructions for performing the job they had been hired to perform. All of his efforts were to no avail. The students simply would not listen. Finally, angry at their inattention and irresponsibility, Hogg fired every single student. It was only later as he collected and counted the lead the students had collected that he realized his mistake. The students had actually collected nearly three times the lead per labor hour as had the cadenced work force. Try as he might, Hogg couldn't get the student crew—the really productive crew—to return to work. Eventually, Hogg lost his contract and spent the rest of his life working in an assembly plant.

How do you ensure that a problem is really worth solving? How do you make sure that what you think is a problem is really a *problem?* Here are some questions to ask to determine if a problem is worth solving as suggested by Robert F. Mager and Peter Pipe in their book *Analyzing Performance Problems*.

1. Does the problem behavior cost the company money either directly (such as when an employee gives a customer the wrong change) or indirectly (such as excessive use of supplies or raw materials)? Calculate exactly how much you think the problem behavior is costing the company per year.
2. Does the problem behavior result in people wasting time because it results in materials shortages, lateness, slow service, or defective work that has to be redone? If time is lost, calculate how much time would be lost in a year and what that loss in time costs the company.
3. Does the problem behavior result in waste or scrap? What is the value of that waste or scrap?
4. Does the problem behavior result in damage to equipment? If so, what is the cost of that damage in repairs or replacement of the equipment?
5. Is there a loss in production as a result of the behavior? If so, what is the value of that lost production?
6. Does quality suffer as a result of the behavior? If so, what is the cost of that loss in quality (in rework, scrap, lost orders, warranty costs, etc.)?
7. Will the problem contribute to an increase in insurance costs as, for example, an increase in insurance premiums due to accidents? What is that cost?
8. Could the behavior result in an increase in accidents or injury on the job? What would be the costs associated with that increase in lost work time, hospital stays, damaged equipment, etc.?
9. Could the behavior result in lost business? If so, what is the estimated value of the business that could be lost?
10. Does the behavior result in duplication of effort? For example, do extra quality checks have to be performed or does it result in two people having to do the work one should be able to perform? What is the cost of that duplication?

11. Does the behavior result in the need for extra supervision or increased administrative support? What is the cost of that extra supervision or support?

Step Three: Decide If the Problem Is a "Won't Do" or a "Can't Do" Problem

When a discrepancy exists between expected performance and actual performance, there really are only two possible explanations for the discrepancy. Either the employee can't do what is expected—doesn't know how to do it—or the employee won't do what is expected even though he or she knows how. No amount of correcting, counseling, discipline, or punishment will solve a "can't do" problem. Provided the employee has the mental and/or physical ability to learn to perform the task, "can't do" problems can only be solved through training, practice, or by changing the nature of the task itself. Thus, before you proceed to holding a correcting or counseling session with an employee about problem behavior, you must determine if the nonperformance is a "can't do" or "won't do" problem. How do you determine what type of problem you are facing? Again, we can turn to the suggestions of Robert Mager and Peter Pipe in *Analyzing Performance Problems*. Ask yourself the following two questions:

1. Could the person perform as expected if his or her life depended upon it?
2. Has he or she ever performed as expected in the past?

If your answer to either of these two questions is no, then the problem is very likely a "can't do" problem you cannot correct through counseling. Look instead for a training solution (see Chapter 4 of this book, on training). If you answer yes to both questions, then it is likely you have a "won't do" problem that you may be able to solve through a counseling session.

Step Four: Decide What Consequences You Are Able or Willing to Use to Correct the Problem

In step three, you determined that you really had a "won't do" problem. Before you proceed to a counseling session with the employee, you must decide what you are willing and able to do to correct that problem. "Won't do" problems usually exist for one or more of two reasons:

1. No feedback—the person doesn't know a problem exists. As surprising as it may sound, often people don't perform according to expectations either because they don't know the expectations or they don't know their performance isn't meeting expectations. In the absence of frequent, data-based, objective feedback on performance, people will often develop misconceptions about their performance. They don't know the score. Since they don't, they assume all is well when it isn't. Obviously, one of the things you will do in your counseling session will be to give the employee verbal feedback on his performance—to correct any misconception he might have about how well he is performing. But what can you do to arrange feedback to that employee about this area of performance on a regular (daily or weekly) basis? In step one, you collect data on performance. Can you arrange to share this data with employees on a regular basis? How would you do that?

2. Nonperformance is rewarding and/or good performance is punishing. Sometimes a "won't do" problem exists because there are a number of positive consequences for nonperformance and few, if any, positive consequences for good performance. For example, Neal may be reinforced for coming in late. He gets to sleep later. He doesn't have to fight rush-hour traffic. He gets to spend more time with his family. He can stay up late and watch the ball game the night before. There are probably many other reasons for Neal deciding that coming late to work isn't such a bad idea. On the other hand, there is probably little in it for Neal to arrive on time. No one is going to thank him for getting to work on time.

He isn't going make any more money for arriving early. In fact, arriving earlier might be punishing to Neal in some ways. We once had a client who had a problem with employees being tardy. As we studied the positive and negative consequences for arriving on time from the employees' point of view, we discovered something very interesting. At this particular company, work assignments were distributed at the beginning of each shift. The first jobs to be assigned were the priority jobs. They also tended to be the most difficult and unpleasant jobs to perform. Employees quickly learned that arriving early meant you got the "dog" assignments. It was much better to come in a little late after the hard work had already been assigned. Then you got the easier, more routine work to do.

In our previous chapter on motivation, we discussed the impact of consequences on employee behavior. We said that consequences—the good and bad things that happen to employees as a result of their behavior—have a powerful and perhaps controlling influence on the behavior. One way to analyze why a behavior is occurring is to examine the "balance of consequences" from the employee's point of view. Here is how you do that:

1. Take a piece of paper and list the problem behavior at the top.
2. Divide the rest of the paper into two columns. Label one column "Positive Consequences" (the good things that happen to the employee when this behavior is performed). Label the other column "Negative Consequences" (the bad things that happen to the employee when this behavior is performed).
3. From the employee's point of view, make a list of all the "Positive Consequences" and "Negative Consequences."

When you complete this exercise, you will often find that, from the employee's point of view, there are many more positive consequences for exhibiting the problem behavior than there are negative consequences. From the employee's viewpoint, coming in late, not maintaining the machine, calling in sick—all of these "problem" behaviors just make sense.

Once you have some understanding of how positive and negative consequences affect employee behavior, your next task is to decide how you can change the "balance of consequences." For example, if Neal is coming in late because there are too many positive consequences for being late, can you add some negative consequences to change the balance? Just how far are you willing to go to change Neal's behavior? After counseling, would you be prepared to fire Neal if his tardiness did not improve? Would you be prepared to dock his pay? On the other hand, are there any positive consequences you can provide Neal for being on time? For example, if his punctuality improves, are you prepared to thank him for correcting the problem? Before you go into a counseling session with Neal (or anyone), you need to decide what action you are prepared to take.

Conducting the Counseling Session

Assuming you have completed the four steps listed above, you are now ready to call the employee in and conduct a counseling session. How you conduct the session itself will determine in large part how successful you are in getting the employee to correct the problem behavior. As we said previously, you have to turn the session into a training session, not a control-oriented confrontation. Here's how you do that.

Counseling Step One: Get Agreement That a Problem Exists

Your first task in a counseling session is to get the employee to admit that he has a problem that is affecting his performance on the job. Let's take the example of Tom, who had not been performing the preventive maintenance on his equipment. Your opening might go something like this:

YOU: Hello, Tom. Have a seat. Tom, do you know why I wanted to talk with you? *(You check to see if he understands that a problem exists. If he does, you can move on to step two.)*

TOM: No.

YOU: Well, I've been checking the maintenance logs and I noticed that you haven't shut your machine down for the scheduled maintenance for the last six months. You can see right here *(show log)* there aren't any entries. *(You pinpoint the problem and share the facts.)*

TOM: Uh—well, we've been so busy and I thought it was more important to get the work out. *(Perhaps Tom doesn't understand the expectations or why the preventive maintenance is so important.)*

YOU: Well, it is important to get the work out, but you know that machine cost us over $100,000, and it won't keep producing the quality our customers expect if it isn't maintained. Also, we have a pretty expensive maintenance agreement on that equipment and it isn't valid if we don't complete the scheduled maintenance. We could end up with some expensive repairs. *(You empathize with Tom's concern for production and then explain the expectations and why they are important to the company.)*

TOM: I see. But I don't see any of the other guys doing all that maintenance. Anyway, nobody told me we *had* to do it any special time, and I don't know why we should have to anyway. We've got stuff to get out. It looks like to me they ought to build these things so you wouldn't have to stop them all the time to do every little thing to them. I got a buddy over at XYZ Company and he says they've got that new Model 40 you don't ever have to shut down . . . *(Watch it here! Tom's getting off the point. He says 'the other guys aren't doing it' so why should he be singled out? Anyway, he says, nobody told him it was that important. And the problem is the kind of machine, not what he is failing to do. You've got to address each of these to move ahead.)*

YOU: Well, Tom, it's not really true that the other guys aren't doing the maintenance. I checked the logs on all the machines, and while I'll admit some of the guys aren't meeting the maintenance schedule like they should, yours has gone the longest without a shutdown for maintenance. I'm going to talk with them also, but here I want to focus on your machine. Now, you say you weren't told about the maintenance? Well, I thought we had given everybody a copy of the maintenance schedule. I'm sorry if you didn't get one. Here, I've got one you can have. *(Give it to him.)* Also, I know that Model 40 is a good machine. We looked into it, but we just can't afford it right now. I guess we're just going to have to keep the ones we have running a little longer. What do you think? *(Show you listened and address his concerns, but get back on the point. The point is Tom performing the required maintenance on his machine.)*

TOM: Well, I guess we oughta do the maintenance if that's what we have to do.

YOU: Good!

Counseling Step Two: Get the Employee to State an Action He Agrees to Take to Address the Problem

In step one, you finally got Tom to agree that a problem did exist and that it was his problem. Now your task is to get him to agree to take some action to remedy the problem. What you want here is a specific commitment, not some vague promise to "take care of it" or "try harder in the future." You might say something like this:

YOU: Tom, we seem to agree that it's important to get the maintenance done on the equipment. *(You paraphrase what he just said—that maintenance was important.)* Now, how can we get the maintenance done on your machine? *(What's his plan to get it done?)*

TOM: Well, we've got a lot of stuff backed up out there—what with me being in here and all. I'm going to have my hands full getting those orders out right now. *(Sounds like Tom is delaying again.)*

YOU: So, the problem is we've got orders backed up and there isn't time to shut your machine down to do the maintenance?

TOM: That's right.

YOU: Well, let's see. How long do you think it would take to get the maintenance done?

TOM: Maybe a couple of hours *(laughs)*. It's been a while.

YOU: And those orders that are backed up, are they all due out today?

TOM: Well, no. I guess not.

YOU: Is there any way we could free up a couple of hours to get the maintenance done?

TOM: Well, I guess we could shift some of the orders over until tomorrow, and Benny, he might help me out by taking a few off my hands while I pull my machine down, I've helped him out before. But I'd need to look over the orders and talk to Benny.

(That's better. Now Tom is agreeing to something specific he can do to get the maintenance done. You're ready to move to step three.)

**Counseling Step Three: Get the Employee
to Agree Upon a Time Frame Within Which
the Action Will Be Taken**

When you have reached this point in the counseling session, you're almost home free. The employee has agreed there is a problem and has a plan to correct it. What remains is to set a time frame for carrying out that plan. Try saying something like this:

YOU: That's sounds like a good plan. When do you think you could look at those orders and talk to Benny?

TOM: Well, I've got the orders out there on the workbench so I guess I could look at them now. And Benny's on break now, I think, but maybe I could catch him when he gets back.

YOU: You think we could get back together in an hour? Would that be enough time for you to talk to Benny and go over the orders?

TOM: I guess so. Yeah, that should be enough time.

YOU: Okay then, you'll take a look at the orders to see which ones we can push over until tomorrow and you'll talk to Benny about taking a few of the rush jobs off your hands. Then you'll get back with me in an hour and we'll see where we stand. Right?

TOM: Right.

When it is conducted in the right way, a disciplinary interview can be a positive, constructive, and educational experience. As in the case of Tom, you clarify expectations, agree upon a plan of action, and set a time for carrying out these actions. A lot of your success in conducting a counseling session depends upon your ability to communicate with employees. In fact, effective communication is essential to high performance in and out of counseling sessions. In our next chapter, we will look at communication as another skill you need to keep your business strong.

_12_

The Art of Communicating

We should all be great communicators. After all, we certainly get enough practice. From the time we are born until the time we die, we are constantly sending messages trying to convey of ideas, desires, thoughts, feelings, needs, and wants to others. With all the practice, you would think we could get our message across. But what happens? Too often, the message we think we send bears little resemblance to the message "they" apparently received. People misunderstand and misinterpret our clearest instructions. It's even worse when they try to communicate with us. Frequently, their messages are unintelligible or barely intelligible. We think we know what they mean. Sure we do. Maybe we do.

Of all the skills of management, the ability to communicate—really communicate—must be the most valuable of all. Without the ability to communicate effectively, we cannot share information, give direction, make decisions, or solve problems. In short, we can't manage. Perhaps more importantly, we can't lead. All great leaders seem to be great communicators. Somehow, they are able to share their vision of the future, inspire their followers, and mobilize people—all with just their words. But what about the rest of us? For us, all too often the simplest message goes awry.

For example, let's consider what happened to Harvey Roberts.

How Communication Broke Down at
Roberts Parts Supply

Things were finally beginning to look better for Harvey Roberts and Roberts Parts Supply that Monday morning. The last two months had been difficult. Orders dropped off. Cash flow slowed to a trickle as major customers delayed payment. But all of that was beginning to change. Just this morning, two major customers paid in full. Plus, after months of trying, Harvey had finally won a major supply contract with West Manufacturing. Then Harvey's phone rang.

RECEPTIONIST: Mr. Roberts, Ben West is on line two.

ROBERTS: Hello.

CALLER: Roberts, this is Ben West at West Manufacturing.

ROBERTS: Good morning, Ben.

WEST: Good morning, Harvey. Listen, the reason I'm calling is about those Model 630 parts we ordered.

ROBERTS: Right, Ben. I was just looking at the shipping order on those this morning. We should have them out to you Thursday, just as scheduled.

WEST: Well that's the reason I called, Harvey. We've got a problem over here. Seems some of my people messed up the inventory record. Now they tell me we're almost out. I'm afraid Thursday isn't going to be good enough on those parts. I'm going to need at least half of that shipment right away. What can you do for me?

ROBERTS: Tell you what, Ben, let me check with distribution and I'll get right back to you. We'll see what we can do.

WEST: Okay, Harvey, I'd appreciate that. *(Hangs up.)*

ROBERTS: Linda, get me Tommy Smith in Distribution.

DISTRIBUTION: Hello, Distribution.

ROBERTS: This is Roberts, let me speak to Tommy Smith.

SMITH: Hello.

ROBERTS: Tommy, where do we stand on that parts order for West Manufacturing?

SMITH: Just a minute . . . yeah, it's right here. We're working on the Parker Electronics order now, then we've got White

Trucking and West. Shouldn't be any problem. We should get the West order out on Thursday as scheduled.

ROBERTS: I don't think that's going to be good enough, Tommy. I just got a call from Ben West and he needs that shipment as soon as you can get to it.

SMITH: Oh. Well, let's see. We could move the West order up before White Trucking. Tell you what, I'll take care of it right away.

ROBERTS: Thanks, Tommy. I knew I could count on you.

(Roberts hangs up and immediately calls Ben West.)

WEST: Hello.

ROBERTS: Bill, I've got good news. I just talked to my guys in Distribution and they're going to take care of your order right away. We'll get it right out to you.

WEST: Thanks, Harvey, I'll tell my people to expect it.

(Five hours later Harvey's phone rings.)

RECEPTIONIST: Mr. Roberts, Mr. West is on line two and he doesn't sound very happy.

ROBERTS: Hello, Ben . . .

WEST: Roberts, what's wrong with you people? You told me you were getting those parts right over to me. It's been five hours. How damn long does it take your guys to drive six blocks?

ROBERTS: Hold on, Bill, there must be some mistake. I'll get right on this, I . . .

WEST: Don't bother. Since you obviously couldn't get the job done, I've already contacted Thompson Parts and they've got a truck on the way. You can just cancel that order we have with you. Thompson's a little more expensive, but at least they deliver. *(Slams down phone.)*

ROBERTS: Linda, get me Smith in Distribution.

SMITH: Hello, Distribution.

ROBERTS: Tommy, what's wrong with you people down there? West just called and chewed me out because they still haven't gotten the parts. You told me this morning you'd get right on it.

SMITH: Wait a minute, Mr. Roberts. I didn't know we were supposed to ship those West parts today. You told me to move 'em up after the Parker Electronics order and that's what we did. We'll be through with Parker tomorrow morning and then do West. They should get them tomorrow afternoon.

ROBERTS: Tomorrow—who said tomorrow? West needed that stuff today. Don't you people ever listen?

SMITH: I'm sorry, Mr. Roberts. I thought you knew we'd be working on the Parker order all day today. Look—uh—if West needs the stuff, we'll stop what we are doing and I'll get my people to put in some overtime. We'll get the West stuff to them the first thing tomorrow morning.

ROBERTS: Never mind—never mind. It's too late. West has already cancelled thanks to you. *(Slams phone down.)*

The Process of Communication

It should be so simple to communicate. We talk; they listen. We write; they read. We ask; they answer. We explain; they understand. It all sounds simple. But it isn't. Consider what really happens when we try to communicate:

Step One: The Message

Communication begins with a thought, an idea, or information we want to send to one another. The thought, idea, information—the message—has meaning to us. It is the meaning we want to send.

Unfortunately, many of us rush to begin communicating before we have fully thought through our message. We begin to speak or write before we have answered three most critical questions: What exactly is the message we want to send? Why do we want to send it? Who do we want to receive it? Even worse, most of us have multiple messages we wish to send, often to the same person and often at the same time. Some of these messages are important. Some are trivial. Some are simple, some complex. Some are routine, some are controversial. In our rush to communicate, we may send all of these messages at once in a confusing, bewildering flow.

Step Two: Encoding the Message

Another problem with the message—the meaning—we want to send is that we can't send it directly. We can't plug their mind into our mind. To convey our message, we have to use symbols—written or spoken words, pictures, sounds, physical gestures, movements. Yet none of these symbols are precise. They never represent a perfect match with the thought, ideas, information, or message we hold in our mind. Although we may try for the exact word or phrase or illustration, inevitably the symbol we choose to represent our thought is less than perfect. Words are a particular problem. We must use words to communicate, but meanings for the words we use are in the people hearing or seeing them, not in the words themselves. And the same word can have so many possible meanings. It has been estimated that the five hundred most commonly used words in the English language have an average of twenty-eight different meanings each. Consider, for example, the many possible meanings of the word *charge*. I can

- Charge you a fee
- Charge your purchase
- Charge the battery in your car
- Charge you with responsibilities
- Charge your horse up a hill
- Get a charge out of your joke
- Place a charge under you and blow you up

I can even charge you with a crime.

Even at this early stage of communication, some of the meaning in our message is lost simply because of the imperfection of language and symbols.

Step Three: The Medium

To convey our message, we must have a medium—a channel or path over which our message will travel from us to them. We speak and sound waves carry our voice to their ears. We write and the paper and ink become the medium. There are hundreds of possible

mediums for carrying our message. Some mediums are personal—
the confidential memo, the private discussion. Some are public—
the announcement in a public meeting, the notice in the company
newsletter. But no medium is neutral. Each adds a "message" to
our message. A whisper carries its own meaning above and beyond
the words whispered. So does a shout. In fact, the medium can
overpower the message. It's true—as the saying goes—"the medium is the message."

If the medium we choose is conversation, the words we use may
have less to do with the message we convey than how we speak
those words and our mannerisms while we are speaking. Many
communication experts believe that as much as 80 to 85 percent
of the real message conveyed in a conversation comes from non-
verbal clues (our expression, posture, tone of voice, and so on)
and not from the words spoken. To test this theory, a communication expert once went through a wedding receiving line smiling,
nodding, shaking hands, and saying, "I shot my husband this morning." Members of the wedding party simply smiled back, shook
hands, and said, "Thank you so much, we're so glad you could
come."

Step Four: Decoding

Before our message can have meaning to the recipient, it must
be decoded. Our listener, reader, employee, customer—the person
to whom we are trying to convey our meaning—must interpret our
words, pictures, gestures. To each, he or she adds meaning—and
not necessarily the meaning we intended. Perhaps the words we
choose don't mean the same to them. Perhaps we have chosen
specialized symbols—jargon, pictures, illustrations—they don't
understand. Perhaps they filter out part of our message so they
hear only what they want to hear. Perhaps, due to noise, they miss
key words. We choose a formal public medium—the public announcement—for convenience. They interpret our choice as
"cold" and "insensitive." Worse, most people are poor listeners.
They become passive—go into neutral—and truly absorb by some
estimates as little as 25 percent of what they hear. While we are
speaking at the rate of 100 to 200 words per minute, they are

thinking at 1,000 to 2,000 words a minute—ten times our speaking rate. With all of that extra time, they begin to jump ahead, make assumptions—fill in what they think we are going to say. They may be rehearsing their response or just daydreaming. As a result, they can miss, mix, or confuse what we have said. We say: "Pick us up on flight 230 at 4:30." They hear: "Come to the airport at 2:30 to meet flight 430."

How to Improve Communication

Given the complexity of communication—even the simplest communication—it is small wonder meaning is sometimes lost. How, then, can you improve the chances of getting your message across? Here are some suggestions.

Think Through Your Message

You will greatly increase your chances of getting your message across if you pause before you speak or write and make sure you can answer the following three questions:

1. What exactly do I want to communicate?
2. Who do I want to receive this message?
3. Why should they listen?

Deciding what you want to communicate means picking the critical elements of the message. What are the key points you want your listeners to remember? Also, what do you expect them to do with this message? Are you giving them information, requesting information, or giving direction? In our earlier story, Harvey Roberts meant to give Tommy Smith direction—"Deliver the West Manufacturing order today." Instead, Roberts requested information—"What is the status of the order?"

Deciding who you want to receive the message is equally important, since the words, examples, how, and when you send the message should be determined largely by your intended audience. You have to send a message audience members will understand

and you have to send it via a medium they monitor. As the saying goes, "Don't send your message on AM if they only listen to FM."

Finally, you have to be able to answer the question, "Why should they listen?" Most people are bombarded with messages. They can't listen to or read everything. Therefore, they are selective. They listen to and read what is relevant to them—what addresses their needs and will help them solve their problems. If you want to get your message across, you have to demonstrate that your message is relevant to your audience. Ask yourself, "How can I present my message in a way that relates to a problem, need, or concern they have?"

Use Only Words, Phrases, and Illustrations You Are Sure Will Be Understood

Most of us recognize that we should avoid using jargon or technical language if we wish to communicate with others. Also, most of us can easily recognize jargon used by others. After all, it is all those words, phrases, and acronyms we don't understand. Yet most of us find it very difficult to recognize our own jargon. Our words, phrases, or illustrations aren't jargon; they aren't too technical—at least not to us. But therein lies the problem. We aren't speaking or writing to "us." We're speaking and writing to "them." And to "them," too often the words we use are jargon. Your English teacher probably told you to write short, declarative sentences if you wanted to get your message across. The same goes for speaking. Constantly ask yourself, "How can I simplify this point and make it more direct?" If the content of your message is technical, ask yourself, "How can I present the same information in a non-technical way?"

Avoid Emotion-Laden Terms

As we said previously, "meaning is in people, not in words." And people react emotionally to their experiences. Most people associate at least some words with prior negative experiences. When you use such words, those negative experiences become associated with your message and, in some cases, overpower your message. Obviously, you can never know every possible word or phrase that might conjure up negative associations, but the more you know about your audience the better off you are. Ask yourself, based upon what you know about your audience, if there are any words or phrases you should avoid.

Tell the Whole Truth and Nothing But the Truth

Your credibility is critical to your ability to communicate. If they can't trust you, they just won't listen or they will misinterpret what you say. If you can't divulge information because it is sensitive or confidential, say so. Lack of trust destroys communication.

Send Your Message Multiple Times in Multiple Ways

You have probably been told not to repeat yourself. This may be the worst possible communication advice. It would be nice if you could send your message only once and have it received. Unfortunately, you can't. There is just too much noise. People are bombarded with messages and it is easy for your message to get lost. If you are in sales, you recognize that rarely do you make a sale on the first contact with a potential buyer. The same is true with communication. You rarely get your message across on the first try. A message sent once and in only one way is likely not to be received. If you are speaking, use a simple diagram or chart to illustrate your main points. If you are issuing written instructions, call a meeting and review the main points of the instructions verbally.

Make Your First and Last Words
Your Most Important

Whether you are speaking or writing, your first and last words are the most critical. Most people look to what comes first and what comes last as a clue to what you are trying to communicate *and* whether they should listen. *Never, never* bury your main points somewhere in the middle. The old rule of "Tell them what you are going to tell them, tell them, and tell them what you told them" is good communication advice.

Listen and Encourage Feedback

Perhaps the most important thing you can do to get your message across is to listen. When you send a message, watch for a response. If your message was received or only partially received, then your listener will respond. No response is a sure sign of "a failure to communicate." It is a signal for you to repeat the message. If there is a response, something was received. But what? It is your responsibility to find out. How? Ask—check on what they heard. Ask a question that cannot be answered with a yes or no. Say, "How do you feel about that?" "What is your opinion?" And so on. Even better, ask them to repeat what they just heard—to rephrase what you said in their own words.

Communication is never easy. Regardless of how simple your message, the danger exists that you will be misunderstood. In this chapter, we have suggested how you can increase your chances of getting your message across. In our next chapter, we will examine a special type of communication—the kind that occurs (or fails to occur) in group meetings. We'll show you how to stop wasting time in meetings and get your message across.

__13__

Successful Meetings

Whether you manage three employees or three hundred, it is inevitable that someday you will have to conduct a meeting. Perhaps you need to share information about a change in company policies or procedures. Or you need to tap the knowledge and experience of some of your key people to gather the facts to support a business plan or to enable you to make a major decision. Maybe you want their input on how to solve a problem with product delivery or customer service. Regardless, you will eventually need to get the "troops" together for a "team huddle."

If your meeting goes well, your troops will immediately march off to implement your new policy just the way you planned; or you'll get the facts you requested to make that major decision; or you'll achieve whatever goal you set out to accomplish at the meeting. But if you are like most business owners and managers, you may find that your meetings just never seem to come off as well as you planned. You try to conduct a meeting and soon the meeting gets totally out of hand. Then when you try to regain control, everyone just sits there grim-faced and quiet. You end up getting angry and preaching to them about taking things more seriously. After the meeting, you overhear two employees talking about how your meeting was just "another waste of time." You have to admit, they just may be right.

The Keys to a Successful Meeting

There are really three key concepts to keep in mind to make every meeting you run a successful meeting.

First, treat every meeting as part of the continuous flow of business operations and communications, not as a one-time event. The success of any meeting is determined not only by the effectiveness of your planning and preparation for the meeting itself, but also by the expectations your employees develop about the role of meetings. Managers who conduct successful meetings develop a type of "meeting culture" where their employees hold positive expectations about the role of meetings in the management of the business. For these employees and their managers, meetings become an important part of "how we operate," "how we coordinate," and "how we get the job done," rather than an "interruption" and "waste of time."

A second key concept for conducting successful meetings is the recognition that meetings involve people interacting in a group setting and that people behave differently in groups than they do one-on-one. Some people are more open and animated, and some act more retiring in a group. The more you know about the participants in your meeting and how they behave in a group session, the more likely you will be able to plan and conduct a successful meeting.

Finally, a key to conducting a successful meeting is to start on time, end on time, and keep the meeting short. Generally, every minute you delay or extend a meeting beyond its schedule, the less effective it tends to be. When you start late, people will get into the habit of arriving late. When you extend meetings past their scheduled ending, people "tune out" as they begin to focus on going home, attending their next meeting, or getting back to their "real" work.

When Not to Conduct a Meeting

Before you conduct your meeting, decide whether you should hold a meeting at all. Meetings often fail simply because they are poorly timed or inappropriate. Recognize that holding a meeting costs the company: it has been estimated that it costs two hundred dollars for ten people making twenty thousand dollars a year to attend a single one-hour meeting. When shouldn't you hold a meeting? Never hold a meeting when a written note, personal phone call, or one-on-one conference would be better. Written communication is more uniform, authoritative, and provides a permanent record. In addition, a written document is more convenient to the writer and the reader. A personal phone call or one-on-one discussion is faster if you must communicate with only a few people and you don't need the benefit of a group discussion. In addition, written notes, phone calls, and personal conversations are more confidential.

If you decide a meeting is the best way to handle a situation or problem, then there is a list of "nevers" that should be met.

- Never hold a meeting without preparation.
- Never hold a meeting if truly key people can't attend.
- Never hold a surprise meeting unless you have a true emergency. Always give people at least two days' and preferably a week's notice of any meeting. Otherwise, expect people to come to your meeting unprepared.
- Never hold a meeting without first making sure that all participants are fully informed about the purpose of the meeting, subject matter to be covered, and exactly what supporting information or data they are expected to bring or be prepared to discuss.

Planning a Successful Meeting

Like most other things, successful meetings start with good planning. Following are some basic steps to heed in planning your meeting.

Step One: Establish the Goal or Goals for the Meeting

Your first task in planning your successful meeting is to decide just what you want the meeting to accomplish. Why are you holding a meeting? Any or all of the following are justifiable and general reasons for holding a meeting:

1. To make a decision. Here, your purpose is to allow everyone who will be affected the opportunity to have input in that decision. What do you want to accomplish? Sure you want a good decision, but whatever the decision, you want support and commitment from the people who will implement the decision.
2. To analyze and solve a problem. Here, you want input from people with different perspectives and access to different facts that have bearing on a problem. Your goal is not just to gain consensus on how to solve a problem, but the benefit of shared ideas, different perspectives, and new pieces of supporting facts.
3. To resolve conflict. You want to get the warring factions together to find some common ground for agreement. Your goal is the resolution of the conflict.
4. To provide information. Here, your goal is to share information that meeting participants can use as a basis for future action. You choose to hold a meeting to emphasize the seriousness of the information, obtain their immediate reaction, and/or to provide an opportunity for questions and clarification.
5. To recognize accomplishments. Your goal is to recognize and reinforce individuals or groups of individuals who have improved performance or contributed to the achievement of company goals.

Step Two: Prepare a List of Specific Agenda Items

Once you have the general reasons for holding the meeting in mind, begin to list specific agenda items. What specific problems do you want to solve? What information do you need to share?

What areas of conflict need to be addressed? Which individuals or groups should you reinforce? Start with a laundry list of items as they come to you. Then list these items in priority. Chances are you will have more items on your list than you can hope to cover in an hour. Therefore, you need to narrow your list. To do so, start at the top of your priority list, estimate how much time you need to allot each item, and stop after one hour. The remaining items will have to wait until next time.

Step Three: Decide Who Should Attend Your Meeting

Once you have the general goal and specific agenda items in mind, you have the information to decide who should attend. Ask yourself, given these agenda items, who

- Has official responsibility for this item
- Must carry out any decision made about this item
- Must approve a decision about this item
- Possesses information about this item
- Can make a unique contribution to our discussion on this item because they have a unique or unusual viewpoint

Based upon your answers to these questions for each item, draw up a tentative list of participants. Then review your list and the agenda items a second time. Do all of these people need to be present for each agenda item? Should you have two meetings instead of one? Can some participants come to just part of the meeting?

Step Four: Draw Up Your Agenda

Your agenda is a plan of what will be discussed in the meeting and the order in which it will be discussed. As you review your agenda items and your list of participants, arrange the items on the agenda to create a natural flow. Since it is hard to abruptly shift the focus of a group from one unrelated topic to another, try to group similar agenda items together to form a natural transition.

Step Five: Select Your "Props"

"Props" are the charts, graphs, diagrams, reports, slides, and so forth you need at the meeting to assist in discussing the agenda items.

Step Six: Select a Meeting Room

There is no such thing as an all-purpose meeting room. If you have a choice of rooms, you should keep in mind the following criteria:

- Choose a room appropriate to the size of the group.
- Avoid a room with windows, or select a room where draperies can be closed and participants are seated facing away from the windows.
- Avoid a long, narrow room.
- Choose a "U" or "horseshoe" arrangement for chairs and tables, or select a room with a large conference table.
- Choose a room with an entrance/exit at the rear of the room (opposite the side participants are facing).

Conducting the Meeting

Your two primary objectives in conducting any meeting should be to keep the meeting focused on the goal(s) and to stay on schedule. Following are some specific suggestions to help you accomplish these objectives:

1. Always begin the meeting by welcoming the participants and briefly summarizing the agenda. Emphasize the goal(s) of the meeting and the results you hope to obtain. Ask for their cooperation and participation.
2. If you are starting a regular series of meetings (for example, regular staff meetings or project review meetings), develop a "code of conduct" during your initial meeting. A code of conduct specifies rules of behavior by which the meetings will

be conducted. Let the participants come up with their own rules. For example, say: "We're going to be meeting like this on a regular basis and I thought one of the first things we might discuss is how these meetings should operate. I would like your ideas about what we, as a group, should do (or refrain from doing) in order to make these meetings more enjoyable and productive. What do you think?" Establish rules such as: "Meetings will start and end on time," "No smoking," "No criticism of others' ideas."

While it sounds simple, establishing a code of conduct from the beginning can be tremendously helpful to you in maintaining order and control at later meetings. If the participants come up with the rules themselves, they will help you to enforce the rules if they are violated.

3. As a rule, limit the time you are talking to no more than fifteen to thirty minutes. Since you want the participants' ideas and opinions you should listen and guide the discussion, not make speeches.

4. To stimulate discussion, ask open-ended questions (those that cannot be answered with a yes or no).

5. To encourage a quiet person to talk, call on them and use their first name. Say, "Jane, what do you think about . . . ?" Reinforce Jane's response by saying: "Thank you, Jane, that was a good point."

6. If a single person or a single point of view begins to dominate a discussion, listen for the person speaking to pause and interrupt them to ask another question. For example, listen for a pause and say: "Thank you, John. Now I'd like to hear what Ted thinks. Ted?" Alternatively say: "Well, I've heard some good reasons why we should not do this. Now tell me some of the advantages in doing it."

7. If the discussion tends to wander off track of the main point, again, listen for a pause from the person speaking and say: "Those are good points, but I think we are getting a little off track. What I'd like us to focus on is how do we . . . ? Mary, what do you think about that?"

8. If you feel you are losing control or need to get their attention, do one or more of the following:

a. Stand up.
b. Walk around the room.
c. Walk to a point where you are standing just behind the person talking or disrupting the meeting.
d. Raise the volume of your voice.
e. Pick up an object (marker, pointer, etc.) and hold it in your hand—yes, that simple act will get their attention.
f. Tap on the table or on the side of a glass or cup.
g. Flip the light switch on and off.

A distraction will usually shift your staff's attention in another direction.

A Meeting With Success

Like most management activities, leading an effective business meeting requires time, effort, and planning. It also requires knowing and applying a few simple but proven techniques. We have tried to suggest some of these skills and techniques in this chapter. An additional benefit that flows from effective meetings is that you begin to create and shape a cohesive team. Building an effective and thorough team, dedicated to making your company succeed, is critical for the success of your business in the highly competitive business climate of the 1990s.

_14_

Overcoming Resistance to Change

Your business must change to survive. If you don't introduce new methods, procedures, and technology, you won't be able to stay ahead of your competition. You have to improve continuously or you'll be left behind. But your business can't improve continuously if your people resist change.

Is it natural and inevitable that your employees will resist change? It often seems that way. How many times have you tried to get your people to learn a new method for performing their work or to use a new technology, only to find that they grumbled and complained, were slow to learn, and reverted to the old method of doing things as soon as they thought you weren't watching? Why do we so often see this "stubborn," seemingly irrational resistance to almost anything new? Is the resistance we see really stubborn and irrational from our employees' point of view? Maybe, but maybe not. Consider how new technology (a new computer system, for example) impacts the workplace.

First, most of us immediately recognize that when we introduce new technology, people are going to have to learn new skills. They are going to have to attend some kind of training to learn how the technology works. Most of us also recognize that people respond differently to the prospect of training, ranging from anticipation to dread.

To a lesser extent, most of us recognize—sometimes only after the technology is installed—that administrative and operating procedures will have to be changed. Seldom are the design and operational requirements of new technology fully consistent with the procedures we have followed in the past. The likelihood is that we will have to issue new administrative or procedural guidelines and people will have to adjust to a new way of doing business. The old way—what we knew by rote, what we followed by habit—isn't valid any more.

Beyond training and new procedures, often we give little further consideration to the implementation of new technology. Our entire plan for introducing new technology may boil down to just in- stallation, training, issuing new procedures, and maybe doing some follow-up and fine-tuning. Too often, we completely ignore other ways the workplace is affected. What other ways? Well, we think there are at least three.

Structural Changes

When you introduce new technology, the formal structure of your organization may change. Authority, responsibility, and for- mal power may be shifted. Some groups and people gain power, others lose power. The nature and type of information available to people can change. Information may become available that was never available before.

For example, in July of 1986, *Time* magazine reported on the boss who never blinks—the boss who can monitor his employees' performance directly from his own computer terminal. When all employees are performing work on the computer, why not? The data is there. Just give the supervisor the ability to punch up an employee and see what's being done. One such software even allows the boss to flash a message—"You're not working as fast as the person next to you." Wouldn't it be nice to know that your boss can precisely monitor everything you do, every minute of the day, every day of the week, forever. Wonderful, isn't it?

Financial Changes—Real or Imagined

Pay scales may change—up or down—as a result of new tech- nology. Now most of us don't mind if it goes up, but what about down? Basic job requirements may change. Incentive and bonus systems may be impacted. Even job security may be threatened. If the technology makes us more productive, does that mean that fewer of us will be needed? If so, who will go first?

Cultural Changes

What once was a high-status, specialized job may no longer be. Isn't the purpose of technology to offset the advantages faster, more capable, more knowledgeable people have? With the new technology, we may now be able to hire less-skilled people. Think about it—what happened when word processors replaced the type-writer? Now it was okay to make mistakes. Speed became more valuable than accuracy, at least the first time around. There was no need to retype the whole page—typos were easy to correct. The new way didn't require much skill.

And the attractiveness of certain groups may change. What was once a high-status, specialized group may no longer have high status. Now any group with the technology may be able to perform what once only the chosen few could do. Isn't that the purpose of technology, after all—to allow all of us to do more things faster and better?

That's a lot of changes—brought about by the new technology. How do employees so often hear about these changes? Consider how Bob Green handled announcing a major change to his employees. He called them all together and said:

> I wanted to get you all together today to tell you that we are going to get a wonderful new technological tool to help us do our jobs faster and easier. Let me tell you what is going to happen—to you.
>
> First, all of you are going back to school. Some of you may think you are pretty good at what you do. But it's a new day. You are all equal. You are all starting over. Now, while you are all learning these new skills, I want you to know that the work we have to do still must get done. We are not going to miss any due dates, and I expect the quality to be just as good.

No concessions. You will just have to find the time to keep up with the work while you learn. Also, we are going to have some new procedures. We are working on them now and will have a detailed, lengthy reference manual for each of you as soon as we get it back from the printer.

Of course, there is going to be a period during which we are doing some of our work with the new technology and some the old way. Now, until we complete the changeover, you should follow the old procedures when you do it the old way, and the new procedures when you do it the new way. And please keep the two straight. We don't want any foul-ups.

Another thing. We will be coming out with a new organization chart. With the new technology, we are going to be able to move some of you people around—sort of shake things up a little. You'll find out what your new job is and who you report to when you see the new chart. Also, we will be changing the way we look at performance. One of the things I'm pleased about is that in the past, there were so many of you that I honestly wasn't quite sure what you were doing every day. Now with this new gadget, I'm going to be able to punch you right up on my screen anytime I want to and see exactly what you've been up to. So you better watch out!

I do have an announcement about your pay. We want to take a look at your positions now that we are going to have this new technology. We just want to make sure we are not paying you more than you're going to be worth.

And one final thing. I understand that there has been a rumor going around that with this new technology we were going to be able to let 30 percent of you people go. Now I want to put the record straight on that one. It is not—I repeat—*not* 30 percent. Now I know all of you are as excited about this new technology as I am. And I know we are all anxious to get trained and get on with it.

Now suppose you worked for Bob. Would you resist the change? Probably—we all would.

Does It Matter If People Resist Change?

People resist change. But what difference does it make? So what if they do resist? If the change is really needed, won't it win out in the end anyway? People have resisted a lot of things in this country, but resistance did not necessarily stop progress. People resisted the Industrial Revolution, but it came anyway. Won't it be the same with the changes we are facing now? Well, maybe. But at what cost? What is the cost of poorly managed change?

First of all, there is a lot of personal anguish when change is poorly managed. There is a lot of organizational turmoil. And the implementation of change is so often significantly delayed. But there is more than that. Well, what do we do? Where do we start to manage the change? Why not start with the people?

Why People React to Change the Way They Do

Let's look at some of the things we know about human behavior—about people and why they react to change the way they do.

First, when implementing change, we must assume that even the most irrational resistance is not seen as irrational by the person who is resisting. You, I, everyone—we react to the world the way we perceive it—based upon our own experience. And the way we react—the way we behave—makes sense from our viewpoint. To us, our behavior is perfectly logical no matter how strange it might seem to someone else. What does this mean for managing change? Well, we think it means that in planning change and managing the resistance to change, we must try to see the proposed change from the viewpoint of the people we are asking to change.

Unfortunately, it means that no one strategy for managing change will work in every instance. Each implementation must be designed and managed only after we have learned as much as we can about the people who will be involved in the change. It also means that when we have the option concerning where to install the change first, selection of the target or pilot group is important. We can increase or decrease the likelihood of success to the extent that we understand the predispositions of the group and individuals we will be asking to change.

A second principle of human behavior that we feel is important is that people react emotionally to change. And their feelings and emotions may be more compelling than their intellect. Also, feelings and emotions change slowly. If we must install the technology where there is considerable opposition, then we can expect that it will take some time for the opposition to subside. People who are emotionally opposed to a change are not going to change their feelings because we tell them to. Preaching is not the answer. They will embrace the change only when they see advantages for themselves in doing so. Thus, any change must include heavy doses of communication—and we mean two-way communication.

In managing change, you should include plenty of opportunities for the people involved in the change to discuss the change and how it is affecting them. They must reach their own conclusions about the advantages of the technology. You can provide support, information, and guidance, but, most important, you must listen.

A third important principle for managing change is that people truly understand only what they have experienced. Their involvement is critical to success. If you are thinking about installing new technology, ideally the people who must use the technology should participate in the decision to acquire the technology in the first place. If that is not possible, then at a minimum they would participate in decisions concerning the implementation of the change. How will training be conducted? How will the technology be installed? What procedures will be changed? How will the technology be first used? The point is that the more people are involved in making these decisions, the less likely you are to encounter significant resistance. In short, people don't resist their own ideas.

A fourth principle of human behavior that we think is important is that whenever you introduce change, you must be concerned not only with its impact on the individual, but also its impact on the work group. People meet many of their personal needs through membership in groups. Acceptance by others is important for most of us. We all like to feel that we are part of something. Groups give us protection and security. They give us identity, recognition, and status. Groups define what behavior is acceptable or unacceptable. The group itself and its leadership—both formal and informal—has a strong influence over members of the group.

If the group as a whole supports the change, then individuals in the group are more likely to go along even if they are personally opposed. On the other hand, if the group and group leaders resist the change, individual members are likely to join in that resistance and the resistance is likely to be stronger. If we are to manage change, we must anticipate the reaction of the group as a whole. We must know the group leaders and anticipate their reaction, since their support is important.

As a final principle of human behavior, we must recognize that in reaching a decision to support or oppose change, people are not necessarily rational. Too often, we assume that given all of the information and alternatives, people will arrive at the same logical conclusion about the advantages of the change that we reached. Yet those who have studied how people reach decisions tell us that even when provided with all of the necessary information, people often ignore much of it.

In reality, rather than amassing information people discard information and simplify choices. Also, we know that people resist making major decisions. In managing change, we think this means that regardless of how open we are in sharing information about the necessity of change, our good ideas may still be resisted. It also means that we may have to focus on achieving the level of change that is feasible rather than the level we all would like. For example, often it may not be feasible to move to the ultimate solution in one step. We may have to proceed in increments. We may have to introduce the change in stages. Rather than trying to introduce all of the capabilities of the technology, it may be better to introduce features one at a time or in logical blocks.

From a training standpoint, we think it is better to introduce first those features of the new method that are easiest to learn and most like the old methods and procedures. And we think it is important for those being trained to have early successes.

To summarize, what we know about human behavior would suggest several things.

First, in planning the introduction of any major change, you should try to assess the impact of the change from the viewpoint of those you are asking to change. You should plan your implementation of change with consideration for the structural, financial, and cultural impact of the change, both as it is in reality and as it is perceived by those who will be affected.

We recommend to our clients that they conduct a "Change Readiness Assessment" for any group targeted for major change. The purpose of such an assessment is to gather information about the concerns of the individuals in the target group, particularly in respect to how they perceive the proposed change affecting them. Based upon this information, we can then design the implementation in such a way as to minimize these concerns. For example, if unfounded fears exist, we can take steps to correct any misconceptions. If employees are concerned about structural, procedural, or other changes that in reality must occur, we can involve them in planning for these changes and phase in these changes to give them time to adjust.

Second, recognize that communication and participation are two of the best methods for overcoming resistance. In planning the implementation of a major change, you should provide adequate time for employees in the targeted group to discuss their experiences with the change. We believe that the group should meet on a regular basis to discuss how the implementation is progressing and that the group should participate in deciding how to resolve any problems that have developed. The information you gain from these discussions will help you identify problems and issues of concern to employees early on. Also, by involving employees in resolving these issues, we feel that you are increasing their ownership of the change.

Third, in respect to group dynamics, we think it is important to obtain the support of formal and informal group leaders. During your assessment, try to identify these leaders and gauge their reaction to the technology. If the leadership is opposed to the technology and you have the option to do so, seek other target groups for your pilot where the group leadership is more receptive. If that is not possible, you should direct considerable effort toward winning the support of the group leaders.

Finally, try to be realistic about change. Be certain that the change is being undertaken for compelling and legitimate business reasons. If that is the case, we believe that any resistance you will encounter can be managed and minimized. However, if the change is being introduced simply because someone in authority wants it, but it is not really needed, it will be difficult and perhaps impossible for you to overcome resistance. In short, it is just very hard to sell people on what is, in fact, a dumb idea.

Assuming the right reason exists for bringing in the technology, we think the best approach is often to introduce the technology in phases. If nothing else, you can structure training so that people have early successes and have time to adjust.

15

Managing and Motivating for Creativity

One of the most important things you can do to ensure the survival and success of your business is to tap the creative power of your people. Chances are someone in your work force has a dynamite idea that might just send your company soaring past your competition. But how do you wrestle that idea to the surface, tame it, and turn it into a money-making idea?

In your company right now, you probably have two types of employees. First, you have what we call the "reluctant creatives." They are the vast majority of employees who never seem to have a new thought or idea—at least they never mention one. We call these employees reluctant creatives because, as we will see, they can be creative if given the right environment. Their problem is just that they are reluctant to express their creative ideas. They need encouragement to be creative. Second, you have a few of what we call the "natural creatives"—those who seem to be bursting with ideas and frequently wreak havoc with everyone else. If only the reluctant creatives weren't quite so reluctant and the natural creatives could channel their explosive energy, then you might really get something done. To tap the creative power of your work force, you need to manage and motivate both types of employees. But how do you do that?

Managing and Motivating the Naturally Creative

What exactly is "creativity" anyway? Most authorities agree that creativity isn't so much the creation of new knowledge as it is the ability of some people to take existing knowledge and use it in a new way. Naturally creative people have the ability to absorb a vast number of seemingly unrelated facts and draw novel conclusions from them. Unlike the rest of us, naturally creative people aren't bound by traditional patterns of thought and traditional approaches to problem-solving. They don't have a restrictive mind-set. To understand how this mind-set can inhibit creativity, try your hand at the following puzzles as a test of your own creativity. If you get stumped, the answers are at the end of this chapter.

CREATIVE PROBLEM-SOLVING PUZZLES

Solving problems requires a creative and free-thinking mind. Many of us tend to look at problems from only one point of view. The following are designed to demonstrate the difficulties we encounter when we attempt to solve problems.

Puzzle One: Connect the Dots

Look at the nine dots below. Your task is to connect all nine dots with four straight connecting lines. Once you place your pencil on the paper, you may not lift it until you have completed the task. The lines may intersect, but you may not go over the same line twice.

· · ·

· · ·

· · ·

Puzzle Two: Supply the Missing Letters

Look at the problem below. There is a rationale as to why some letters are on the top and some are on the bottom. Your task is to determine why the letters are arranged as they are. Once you do this, you will know where other letters of the alphabet should be placed. Write in the next two letters in the sequence.

$$\text{B} \qquad \text{C} \qquad \text{D}$$

$$\text{A} \qquad \text{E} \qquad \text{F}$$

Puzzle Three: A Problem in Mathematics?

Look at the problem below. Under each of the single digit numbers 4, 5, 6, and 8 there are two-digit numbers. Your task is to figure out the pattern and by doing so place the correct number in the blank space under the number 7.

4	5	6	7	8
61	52	63		46

If you had trouble completing these puzzles, you are not alone. Most people do. Why? Because the solutions to these puzzles require that we break out of traditional patterns of thought. For example, if you had trouble with Puzzle One it was probably because you tried to keep your lines contained within the confines of the square formed by the dots. But the instructions said nothing about staying within the square. Go back and try the puzzle again. This time, give yourself the freedom to extend your straight lines out well beyond the square. If you had a problem with Puzzle Two, maybe it was because you tried to solve it by looking for an order or sequence in the letters. Go back and try this puzzle again. This time, think in terms of shapes. If you had trouble with Puzzle Three, try doing something more than just adding, subtracting, muliplying, or dividing to get the answer. Think about the order of the digits in your answer.

Did these suggestions help? Chances are you solved the puzzles or got closer to a solution. Why? Because you tried an alternative way of looking at the puzzles. Naturally creative people do this all the time. In fact, the fun to them comes from approaching prob-

SOME FACTS ABOUT CREATIVE PEOPLE:
DID YOU KNOW . . . ?

Imaginative and creative people are often not recognized by their contemporaries. History is full of illustrations. Consider some of these:

- Einstein was four years old before he could speak and seven before he could read. Someone once said of him: "He doesn't wear socks and forgets to cut his hair. Could be mentally retarded."

- Beethoven's music teacher once said of him: "As a composer, he is hopeless."

- A well-known magazine editor told Emily Dickinson her poems were unpublishable because they failed to rhyme.

- When Thomas Edison was a boy, his teachers told him he was too stupid to learn anything.

- F. W. Woolworth got a job in a dry goods store when he was twenty-one, but his employers would not let him wait on a customer because he "didn't have enough sense."

- A newspaper editor fired Walt Disney because he had "no good ideas."

- Louisa May Alcott was told by an editor that she could never write anything that had popular appeal.

lems in unique ways. Their minds travel in many directions searching for answers. They try many different approaches to seek a solution. The rest of us are structured, logical, and frequently judgmental. They are unstructured, intuitive, and open to new ideas. For us, problems are something to be avoided. For them, a problem is a new opportunity. Often, they see a problem where we see none. They question the validity of our most widely accepted notions about how things work or should work. They pepper us with "silly" questions that often begin with the word *Why*. Then they challenge our pat answers and assumptions. Naturally creative

- Winston Churchill failed the sixth grade and failed the entrance exams to Sandhurst twice before he finally passed. He did not become Prime Minister of England until he was sixty-two, and then only after a lifetime of defeats and setbacks. His greatest contributions came when he was a senior citizen.

- Henry Ford failed and went broke five times before he finally succeeded.

- Eighteen publishers turned down Richard Bach's 10,000-word story about a "soaring" seagull, *Jonathan Livingston Seagull*, before Macmillan finally published it in 1970. By 1975, it had sold more than 7 million copies in the U.S. alone.

- Colonel Sanders was considered too old to start a business.

- An "expert" said of Vince Lombardi: "He possesses minimal football knowledge. Lacks motivation."

- Gertrude Stein submitted her poems to editors for twenty years before she had one accepted.

- Sam Walton's ideas for a discount store were rejected by executives at Ben Franklin as totally unworkable. Unconvinced, Walton went out on his own to form Wal-Mart. He became one of the most successful retailers in the country.

people are so different from the rest of us that we often find them difficult to work with and manage. To our later regret—we may have such difficulty with them that we miss the opportunity to benefit from their ideas. History is full of examples of naturally creative people who became famous for their ideas only after a lifetime of rejection (see some famous examples in the above box).

How can we manage and motivate the Albert Einsteins, Sam Waltons, Henry Fords, and Walt Disneys of the world? Here are some ideas.

Don't overload your staff with creative people.

Every business needs some people to be creative most of the time and most people to be creative some of the time. But, except in rare instances, few businesses need everyone to be creative all of the time. The routine, boring, day-do-day things have to get done. If you overload your staff with the naturally creative types, you do a disservice to your company and a disservice to your naturally creative people. Every staff and every business needs some free thinkers and dreamers, but if you have nothing but that, chances are you have a problem. Try spreading your creative types around by using them to seed less creative groups or rethink your staffing needs.

Provide your naturally creative people with freedom and structure.

If your naturally creative people are to flourish, you have to give them time and room to think, explore, question—time to create. But don't lose sight of the fact that you have a business to run. You have to produce a product, provide services, and satisfy customers. Thomas Edison once said that creation was "1 percent inspiration and 99 percent perspiration." The danger with your naturally creative types is that they will become so enthralled with the "inspiration" side that they will never get to the "perspiraton" side of putting their ideas to work. It is up to you to provide the structure to keep them on schedule and to let them know when it is time to "stop creating and go with what we have."

Provide each naturally creative person with the right environment.

Some naturally creative people perform best when allowed to work on their own. Others need the stimulation that comes from being part of a group. There is no way to know in advance which environment works best for which person. You have to try them out and observe what happens. By observing them in different settings, you will be able to steer them to their best environment.

Make "time to create" the "carrot."

Naturally creative people enjoy the creative aspect of their jobs. It is what they want to do. If left alone, they will neglect the routine and "boring" to do nothing but create. Maybe some of the routine and "boring" aspects of their jobs can be neglected, but not all. Reports have to be written. Work must be documented. Administrative paperwork must be completed. Customers have to be served. Routine things must be done if your business is to function. Be flexible with your naturally creative people. Give them time to be creative. But insist that they perform the critical routine and boring stuff first. Then, and only then, can they create. "Creating" is the dessert.

Invest in communication.

You should spend a good portion of your time communicating with all of your employees. But communication is particularly important with your naturally creative types. Perhaps more than any other type of employees, they need to understand your business and business demands so they can turn their natural skills to solving your real business problems. If left to their own devices, naturally creative people frequently will become obsessed with trivia. They'll spend enormous amounts of time and money solving problems that won't pay off for you or the company. Instead of letting them waste your time and their time, provide them with information and direction. Define a real problem for the company for them to work on, and turn them loose. You may be surprised at the results. But be careful: make sure it is a real problem. If it is "make work," they'll recognize it as such.

Provide your creative people with reinforcement and support.

Naturally creative people often appear to the rest of us to require little, if any, external reinforcement for what they do. They appear to be sustained by the mere act of creation itself. Plus, they are so creative so often that we begin to ignore their creative efforts.

What would be extraordinary from someone else is ordinary and expected coming from them. Yet it shouldn't be. Naturally creative people are no different from your other employees in respect to their need for praise and recognition for the results they produce. They might not readily admit that they need your support, but they do.

Managing and Motivating the Reluctant Creative

Your naturally creative employees are a valuable resource for unique and novel ideas. But if you ignore the creative potential of the rest of your employees, you may miss your greatest reservoir of novel ideas. Sure, these employees aren't usually creative. However, they can be. Ample research exists to show that practically every person can be creative regardless of intelligence, age, sex, or education. Why, then, aren't most people creative, and what can you do to tap the creativity of the "normal" person?

Earlier in this chapter, we noted that a significant difference between the naturally creative person and the rest of us was that they approached problems with a different mind-set. In contrast, most of us are locked into traditional thought patterns and processes. We follow the tried and true. We have been taught or have learned from experience that the way to solve a problem or confront something new is to relate it to a previous experience. What have we previously encountered like this and how did we respond? If our solution worked before, maybe it will work again. We compartmentalize and categorize problems and situations. For each type of problem or situation, we apply our preformulated, tested solution. And it usually works. It's not creative, but it is effective and efficient. Plus, it helps us to retain our sanity in an often confusing world. So what's wrong with that?

The problem with our traditonal approach to new situations and new problems is that we tend to jump to solutions before we fully understand the new problem. We end up applying the right solution to the wrong problem. A classic example of this occurred in a large corporation. Managers of this company discovered that customer orders weren't being filled on time. They jumped to the conclusion that their employees needed training, and they spent thousands of dollars on a new training program. Yet even after the extensive training, orders were still not filled on time. It was only after the money had been spent that an enterprising employee suggested that employees were making mistakes and taking too long to fill orders because the order bins weren't always located in the same place. "Why not," he suggested, "paint the order bins different colors according to product line so employees could easily find what they needed?" His suggestion was adopted and performance improved almost immediately. His "creative" solution was quick, effective, and inexpensive. But no one had thought of it before.

In another company, managers noticed that the plant floor was cluttered with product. They jumped to the conclusion that the company had too much work-in-process inventory and implemented a Just-in-Time inventory system at great expense. Only later did they discover the real problem. The clutter on the plant floor was actually rework and rejects due to poor quality. What they needed was better quality control.

Helping the Typical Employee to Be Creative

There are three things you can do to help your typical employee express his or her creative ideas.

Involve your employees on a group basis in finding creative solutions to business problems.

Repeatedly research has shown that people develop better and more creative solutions to problems when they work together in a group. One advantage of group problem-solving is that employees build upon each other's ideas. One idea suggests another idea. That idea suggests still another. As the sequence of ideas progresses, typically the ideas presented get better and better. Another advantage of working in a group is that participants are more accepting of and committed to the final solution. In short, people are much more likely to support and implement an idea they helped develop.

*In group problem-solving efforts, you should always
start with an exploration of the causes of a problem
rather than its possible solutions.*

Most employees will jump to offering solutions to a problem
before it is fully defined. At this stage, the solutions they offer will
be traditional tried-and-true ones that are not very creative. Plus,
when you don't spend time looking for all possible causes, employees may develop solutions for the wrong problem. You greatly
increase your chances of breaking mind-sets and developing creative solutions if you force your employees to start with a search
for causes, not solutions.

*Use one more of the following group problem-solving
techniques to create an environment where people are
free to express their ideas.*

Most people can be creative. But most people are reluctant to
express their creative ideas because they fear their ideas will be
ridiculed and/or rejected. Since no one wants to appear foolish,
most people stay silent when asked for a suggestion, or else they
make a suggestion they are confident will be accepted. All of the
following techniques for group problem-solving, at least in part,
are designed to break down this barrier to creativity. In most cases,
they do so by creating an environment in which ideas are not
evaluated as they are presented. No one is allowed to say "That
won't work." Additionally, these techniques are designed to remove personal ownership and identification with individual ideas.
During the process, the presenter of the idea becomes anonymous
and the ideas become the group's ideas. As a result, when the
ideas are evaluated and some are rejected, the rejection carries
no personal stigma.

Brainstorming

Let's start with one of the oldest techniques for helping people
to be creative—brainstorming. It was developed in the 1950s and
used originally in advertising. Brainstorming assumes that one of

the important reasons most people don't express their creative ideas is that we tend to evaluate ideas as they are presented. Since most ideas we have are not "great ideas" when we first think of them, we sit silent. Few of us want to suggest a new, unproven, innovative idea only to be met with "Won't work"; "We can't do that"; or "We tried that—didn't work." Recognizing that such comments kill ideas, the developers of brainstorming suggested, "Why not separate idea generatoin from evaluation?" If we had the freedom to throw out ideas in a group without the fear of having our ideas criticized, then maybe more people would suggest ideas. Plus, we might be able to build off each other's ideas. Listening to one crazy idea after another, someone might eventually put one crazy idea together with another crazy idea and come up with something unique that really would work.

As we said, brainstorming has been used successfully to encourage creativity for over thirty years. However, to make it work for you, you must follow some simple rules:

1. Choose a topic to brainstorm that isn't too broad or too narrow. For example, "What causes bad quality?"; "How can we make customers like us?"; "What new use could our customers make of product X?" These are all good brainstorming topics.

2. Brainstorm the causes of a problem before you brainstorm possible solutions to a problem.

3. Brainstorming works best if you restrict the size of the group to six to twelve people. That is enough people to generate a lot of ideas, but not so many that everyone can't participate.

4. To lead a brainstorming session effectively, you have to be something of a cheerleader. You have to make the process fun and encourage the more reluctant in the group to participate. The more relaxed you are, the more relaxed the participants will be and the more ideas you will generate.

5. Go over the five basic rules with the group in advance:
   a. No one is allowed to criticize an idea.
   b. Go for quantity, not quality—the more ideas the better.
   c. Everyone should participate.
   d. "Freewheeling" is encouraged—the crazier the ideas the better.

  e. Combine and build upon each other's ideas.
6. Use a flip chart to record ideas rapidly as they are presented. Have one or two recorders to help you in writing up the ideas.
7. Keep the whole brainstorming session moving rapidly. Praise the people for the volume of ideas. ("That's great! We've got a dozen. Let's go for another dozen.") Note: Never praise a particular idea.
8. If necessary, to get things going or to encourage more ideas, offer a "crazy" idea of your own.

Brainstorming has been repeatedly shown to be an effective technique for generating a lot of ideas in a very short period of time. If the problem or issue being brainstormed is broad enough, it is not unusual for a good brainstorming session to generate fifty or one hundred ideas within as little as an hour. Obviously, many of these ideas are unworkable or unusable, but five or ten will be and it is those five or ten that make the whole process worth the effort.

In addition to brainstorming, there are numerous more recent methods for encouraging employee creativity. The following are just a few examples.

The "Random Word" Method

Here, you pick a word at random and brainstorm its association with a problem or issue you are considering. In fact, a major soup company used this method of brainstorming to come up with a new line of soups. They started with the word *handle*. What did that have to do with soup? *Handle* made someone think of *utensil*. *Utensil* suggested *fork*. *Fork* suggested *eat with a fork*. Thus, "Chunky Soup" was born, the kind you can "eat with a fork."

The Picture Method

Works the same way as the "random word" method, but you start with a picture and see what it suggests.

The "Slip" Method

Here, instead of shouting out an idea, everyone is given slips of paper to write down their ideas. The slips of paper with the ideas are collected and the ideas are posted for discussion. This method is particularly good if the problem is not likely to result in a lot of ideas or if people have been reluctant to express their ideas verbally in previous brainstorming sessions.

Brainwriting

This is similar to the "slip" method, but in this case people write their ideas on full-size sheets of paper and then pass the paper to the next person, who tries to build upon that idea.

Card Posting

Similar to brainwriting, but instead of passing sheets of paper on to the next person, individuals write their ideas in large letters on a 5″ × 8″ card and post the card on the wall (with tape) as they finish them.

Nominal Group Technique (NGT)

Developed by Andre Delbecq and Andrew Van de Ven at the University of Wisconsin in 1968, NGT is a process that not only generates ideas but also leads to consensus on the best of these ideas. First, participants are given a formal problem statement printed at the top of a blank sheet of paper. They are given ten to fifteen minutes to generate their ideas "silently" in response to the problem statement. No talk is allowed. Second, each person in turn is asked to read one of his or her ideas out loud to the group. A recorder writes the idea on a flip chart page. This round-robin phase continues until all ideas have been presented. Then each member of the group is asked to pick what he or she feels are the five best ideas and write these on a 3″ × 5″ card, one idea to a card. Fourth, each participant is asked to assign a rank from 1 to 5 for each of the ideas. Finally, the cards are collected and the rankings are tabulated.

Putting Your Ideas to Work

With the exception of the Nominal Group Technique, none of the methods for generating creative ideas we just mentioned result in the selection of an idea(s) for implementation. When you use these techniques, you end up with a list of possible causes of a problem and/or possible solutions to a problem. Whether you are working on causes or solutions, obviously you need to reach consensus on one or a small number of creative ideas to pursue. The ranking and voting procedure in NGT is an excellent method for reaching this consensus and can be used with any of the techniques we have mentioned. If you still have problems reaching agreement, try taking one idea at a time and having the group brainstorm the pros (advantages) and cons (disadvantages) of implementing that idea. Usually, when people make a list of the pros and cons, consensus will emerge.

Regardless of how you reach consensus, you must move to action. You do this with an action plan. Essentially, an action plan is nothing more than a list of who will do what by when. But it is critical. Many creative solutions to problems—whether developed through a group process or by a naturally creative individual— never result in benefit to a company simply because there is no follow-through to implementation. Don't let that happen. Develop an action plan and try it out. Taking action is the "perspiration" and, to paraphrase Edison, perspiration is 99 percent of creativity.

SOLUTIONS TO THE CREATIVE PROBLEM-SOLVING PUZZLES

Puzzle One: Connect the Dots

To solve this puzzle, try extending your lines beyond the confines of the square formed by the dots. There are many possible solutions. One is shown below.

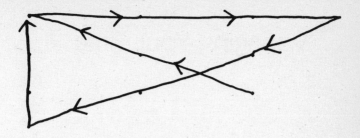

Puzzle Two: Supply the Missing Letters

To solve this puzzle, think about the shape of the letters. Letters on the top row are all made with curved lines. Those on the bottom are made with straight lines. Therefore, the next two letters in the alphabet (G and H) would be placed as follows:

B   C   D   G

A   E   F   H

Puzzle Three: A Problem in Mathematics?

To solve this puzzle, you must multiply the top number by itself and then reverse the digits in your answer to get the bottom number. Notice that 4 × 4 = 16, reversed is 61; 5 × 5 = 25, reversed is 52; etc. Therefore, 7 × 7 = 49, reversed is 94.

4   5   6   7   8

61   52   63   94   46

_16_

Managing Your Time

Where does the time go? It is three hours since your last employee left for the day. You are still sitting in your office with a stack of work to do. The financial records your accountant sent over this morning still sit in your side chair where you dropped them. You planned to review them first thing, but never even got time to open the envelope. Right now, you are working on that estimate for Bryce Electronics that was due yesterday. How could you have forgotten that it was due? You meant to start on it three days ago, but then there was one thing after another and you just never got to doing the estimate. Now you know you are going to be here well after midnight. When you are running a business, there is just never enough time. In this chapter, we offer some suggestions for managing the time you do have available.

Develop Your "Time Budget"

Everyone has the same amount of time—all the time there is. If you are constantly running out of time, it isn't the lack of time, but your use of time that is the problem. You really can't manage time and you can't create more time. What you can do is manage how you use the time you have. To do that, you need a plan. In fact, you need two plans—one long term and one short term.

For your long-term plan, you need a "time budget." Like any budget, your time budget is your plan for how you will spend a valuable resource—in this case, your time. To create a time budget, you first need an inventory of demands on your time. You need to itemize your expected time expenditures. To do so, take a ledger sheet and divide it into six columns. Label the columns as follows:

1. Daily
2. Weekly
3. Biweekly
4. Monthly
5. Quarterly
6. Yearly

Under each heading, list recurring activities you must perform according to their frequency, together with an estimate of how much time you need to allot to each activity. For example, you might have to make bank deposits. List *bank deposits* under the daily column with an estimate of how much time this takes, say two hours. Weekly, you might have to prepare the payroll and sign payroll checks. List *payroll* under the weekly column with an estimate of how much time it takes you to prepare the payroll. Continue until you have all of the recurring activities you can recall. To get a more accurate list, try keeping a daily time log for one or two weeks.

Once you have a complete list of recurring activities, review this list to see if you can delegate any items (or part of items) to others. For example, if you normally prepare the payroll all by yourself, could you delegate part of the work to an assistant? Perhaps Mary, your secretary, could complete the time sheets and total the hours. She could then submit them to you for review and final approval. How much time would you save? Make a note on your list to train Mary to perform initial work on the payroll and reduce your estimate of the time you must spend accordingly.

Your ability to delegate successfully is key to your success in completing this step in preparing your time budget. In a later chapter, we will discuss delegation in more detail. For now we will only note these key points to remember when you delegate a task.

1. Pick a person to perform the task who has the basic aptitude *and* who is motivated to perform it.

2. Invest in training. Plan to take the time necessary up front to ensure that he or she acquires the necessary skills to complete the task successfully.

3. Use a try-out period. Instead of delegating the entire task, begin with delegating just a portion of the task. Once they are successfully performing this first small part of the task, add other parts until they can eventually perform the entire task. With a try-out period, you minimize your risk—there is less they can do wrong—and you increase the likelihood of their success since they learn to complete the task in small stages or steps.

4. Finally, be patient. No one will perform the task exactly right the first time, and they will probably never perform the task exactly the way you do. Remember, it is the timely and accurate completion of the task that is important, not necessarily the precise execution of steps according to your personal "one best way."

Now you have a list of recurring activities reduced by those tasks you have decided you can delegate. Your next step in developing a time budget is to transfer this information to a calendar. Any type of calendar will do, but you will probably find it easier to work with a large daily or weekly format.

Your calendar is a visual picture of the time available to you. All of the recurring business activities you have listed, plus nonrecurring activities, have to fit on this calendar. In addition, you have to allow for your personal time—to sleep, eat, be with your family, enjoy the holidays, take that vacation you've been putting off. As you review your business list and the time you need for your personal life, don't be surprised if your "large" calendar appears to shrink. Now you are beginning to face the real problem. There is just so much time available. You have precisely 24 hours a day, 168 hours a week, and 8,736 hours a year. While that may seem like a lot, it isn't. Take away 7 hours to sleep, 2 hours to eat, 1 hour to dress, 1 hour to commute to your business, and as little as 2 hours a day for family and personal chores; and suddenly over half of your available time is gone. Deduct a little more time to read, enjoy a hobby, engage in a sport, exercise, or have just a little free time to get away from it all, and you have 40 hours, or 50 hours—60 hours a week at the most—to devote to your business. It is during those hours that you must accomplish your business tasks.

How much time are you willing to devote to running your business? Perhaps your business is young and you are prepared to sacrifice more of your personal time to your business, at least for the first few years. Perhaps your business has matured and you now want to cut back on your business commitments to provide more time for family, friends, or leisure. Now is the time to make your decision. Cross out blocks of time on your calendar that you plan to reserve for your personal life. The time that remains is your total business time budget. Within this budget, you must plan for your recurring activities and still leave at least half of your business hours (or more) available for nonrecurring activities.

To fill in your business calendar, begin by allocating time for the recurring activities you have listed. For example, if you need two hours a week to prepare the weekly payroll, block out that time on your calendar when it must occur. In recording your recurring activities, first enter those that have specific deadlines, then enter other activities that can be performed at any time during the day, week, month, etc. Also, try to reserve the first and last half hour of each day and approximately 50 percent of the total time for nonrecurring tasks, since you will need these blocks of time for your daily (short-term) plan.

Your Short-Term Plan or Daily "To Do" List

Your time budget is your long-term plan. It covers predictable or recurring tasks that you must complete. It also reserves time for nonrecurring tasks. These are the real time robbers. If you don't get control of these unanticipated, day-to-day tasks, they will eventually consume all of your time. The two hours you allocated in your time budget to work on the payroll will disappear as you deal with one crisis after another. How do you get control of these nagging time robbers? You do so with your short-term plan or daily "To Do" list.

As its name implies, your daily "To Do" list is a simple, prioritized list of nonrecurring things to accomplish each day. What kinds of tasks are these?

- Phone calls you have to return
- Reports you have to write
- Meetings you have to conduct
- Visits with customers

Include all of those things that occur only once or that you can't plan for on a long-term basis. You have to plan for these tasks on a daily basis. When? During the first and last half hours of each day.

You will recall from building your time budget that we suggested you reserve the first and last half hours of each day for nonrecurring activities. You should prepare, review, and revise your daily "To Do" list during these two half hours each day. During the last half hour, you review your "To Do" list for the upcoming day. Move over to the next day's list any items you have not completed and also add any new items. Then prioritize your list by picking out the five most important items and number them from 1 to 5 in priority order. Don't be concerned if your list of "To Do" items is long. It is likely that you will never complete all of the tasks you can list for any single day. Completing all of the tasks you list is not important. Having a list and completing the top five (or just the top item) *is* important.

When you have completed your list and picked at least your top five items, go home—and take the list with you. At night, if you think of an item, add it to the list. The key to gaining control over these nonrecurring activities is to get them on your list. If you are away from the office and don't have your list with you, phone in a message (to your receptionist or answering machine) to remind yourself to add an item to your list when you return.

One way to build your "To Do" list and ensure you don't forget an important item is to set aside time each day to quickly scan your mail, fax messages, phone messages, and internal memos.

As you review each item, make a brief note on the item concerning action you need to take (i.e., "Call John and discuss this," "Do estimate for this," "Write reports"). Then add the item to your "To Do" list. Don't try to complete any of these items at this time.

Earlier, we suggested that you set aside the first half hour of each day for nonrecurring activities. This first half hour is critical. During this time, you use your "To Do" list and time budget calendar to plan your day. Review your "To Do" list and transfer at least your top five priority items to your time budget calendar, filling in time for each item from the "To Do" list around the time you have already set aside for recurring activities such as preparing the payroll. For the remainder of the day, try to work off your completed time budget calendar for that day.

Handling Interruptions

If you follow your time budget and work on priority items off your "To Do" list, you will make maximum use of the time available to you. You won't accomplish every task you can identify, but you will accomplish the most important. But you must follow your plan. To do so, you must handle interruptions—anything that will cause you to depart from your plan. Unexpected phone calls, drop-in visitors, and business crises are all notorious interruptions. Here are some general rules to follow to minimize interruptions.

Plan for Interruptions

No plan is ever perfect. Therefore, it is wise to plan for some interruptions. When working out your time budget, set aside an hour or so each day to deal with the unexpected. Try increasing your estimates of time to complete each task by 10 or 20 percent to allow for interruptions. When you delegate a task—particularly when a person is first learning the task—set a target date for completion of the task a day or two prior to when the task must be completed. The extra time will give you a chance to review the work and accomplish any required revisions.

Manage Your Telephone Usage

While your telephone can be a big time saver, it can also rob you of much of your valuable time. To manage phone usage, do the following:

- Set aside telephone time. Make or receive phone calls only during these hours.
- Have someone screen your calls. Have them take messages except from those key individuals you need to speak with immediately.
- Avoid the temptation to respond to telephone messages in the order they were received. Instead, review all of your messages once or twice a day and return calls in priority order. Whenever possible, delegate the task of returning a call to someone else.
- Install a cellular phone in your car and use time in transit to make some of your calls.
- If you just need to send a message, confirm an appointment, or anything else for which a two-way exchange isn't necessary, try faxing a short message rather than making a phone call.
- Equip your phone system with a switch that allows you to turn off the bell on your office phone. Route all calls through your receptionist.
- When you call someone, be pleasant, but tell them you don't want to waste their time, so you'll get right to the point of the call.

Manage Meetings

Try the following to make maximum use of your time in meetings:

- Don't have a meeting in your office. Hold your meetings in a conference room or go to another office. That way you can leave the meeting whenever you want.
- Have an agenda for all formal meetings and stick to it. For informal meetings, jot down your key objectives in advance

(i.e., "Why do you need to see this person?") and try to stick to them.

- Have a time limit for each meeting (preferably an hour or less), and stick to it. If you cover your priority items first and time runs out, the remaining items can usually be postponed to another meeting.
- Keep the number of participants in any meeting to a minimum and ensure that each person attending knows the agenda in advance and why they are attending.

Manage "Drop-in" Visitors

People who visit your office unexpectedly can consume an enormous amount of your time. To keep these visits to a minimum, try the following:

- Place a "Do Not Disturb" sign on your door when you don't want to be interrupted.
- Stand up when someone enters your office, and meet them at the door. If you and your visitor remain standing, the meeting will likely be shorter. Alternatively, have no side chairs in your office (so there is no place for visitors to sit), or keep books and papers in your side chairs. If you want visitors to sit down, you can always get a chair or remove the books and papers.
- Many drop-in interruptions occur because people who report to you are unclear about their assignments. To avoid such interruptions, have a short (half-hour) meeting with your key staff at the beginning of each day to quickly review the day's activities. Resolve any questions at this time.

Use the "Two-Step Process" for Handling Paperwork

While you may have heard the saying "Handle each piece of paper only once," it is often bad time-management advice. Why? Because you may end up handling low-priority paperwork while high-priority items wait. Instead, use the two-step process.

Step One: Scan all of your paperwork and note what must be done. Sort the work into three piles—high, medium, and low priority.

Step Two: Work on high-priority items first, then medium, and finally low. It is during Step Two that you should handle each piece of paper only once.

Another way to remain focused on the high-priority items is to remove other items from your desk. Place them in a file, drawer, or other container so you can't see them and, consequently, can't be tempted to work an item out of order.

__17__

How to Delegate

Of all the things you can do to make your business a success, perhaps the most important is to stop trying to do everything yourself. If you are not delegating to your staff, you may destroy your business in the long term. Yes, it's true. Your hard work, the long hours you put in, and your personal attention to every detail may be hurting—not helping—your business. Almost inevitably when we have seen a business fail, a major (or at least contributing) cause of the failure was the inability or unwillingness of the owner or a key manager to delegate. Tragically, many of these businesses failed just at the point where they were really taking off. Orders were pouring in. Customers were lined up at the door. But the owner tried to do everything—check every order, serve every customer, make every decision. Then quality began to slip. Delivery dates were missed. Customer service deteriorated. Why? Because there was just too much work for one person and the employees hadn't been trained or motivated to share the load.

In this chapter, we focus on delegation—how to determine if you have a delegation problem and what to do about it if you do.

Do You Have a Delegation Problem?

Do you have a delegation problem? Answer the following questions with a yes or no, then count the number of yes answers you give. Later, we will show you how to interpret the results.

153

1. Are you working longer and longer hours with less time for your family and friends?
2. Are you reluctant to take a vacation for fear that your business might suffer in your absence?
3. Do you feel you must constantly double-check your employees' work to make sure it is done right?
4. Do you get upset when things aren't done your way?
5. Do you constantly complain about how hard it is to find "really good people" to work for you?
6. Do you seem to always be "putting out fires"?
7. Do you find yourself doing things because "it's just easier to do it yourself than to try to tell them how to do it"?
8. When you do give an order or make an assignment, do you find yourself spelling out every detail of what should be done and how it should be done?
9. Do you frequently carry work home with you because there just isn't enough time to get it all done during the day?
10. Do you feel constantly under pressure with too many things to do?
11. Do your employees frequently check with you about how to perform routine work?
12. Do you feel it necessary to issue reams of written policies, procedures, rules, and guidelines to cover every conceivable issue and situation?
13. Do you insist that "no money is to be spent" without your approval?
14. Do you feel uncomfortable if you don't know the technical details concerning how to perform the jobs of the people who report to you?
15. Do you find it hard to set priorities and seem instead to jump from one thing to another throughout the day?
16. Are you cautious about how much information you can share with your employees, preferring instead to just tell them "what they need to know"?
17. Does your business often seem disorganized and chaotic?
18. Do you find it difficult to directly supervise more than three or four people because "there just isn't enough time"?

How did you do? If you answered yes to more than three or four of these questions, then chances are you need to improve your delegation skills.

Why Should You Delegate?

All right, suppose you don't delegate as much as you could. What difference does it make? Sure, some day the business might get too much for you to handle, but right now you get by. Of course, you have to put in sixty or seventy hours a week, but you love the business—every detail of it. It isn't as if you are doing something you don't want to do.

There are two good reasons to start to delegate now. First, delegation will help you develop and retain the kind of staff that every business needs for success today. When you delegate, your employees become more knowledgeable and flexible. With increased knowledge, they can provide better service to your customers. Their increased flexibility means an ultimate reduction in your labor costs since each employee will be able to perform a variety of tasks rather than just a few narrowly defined specialities. You also have a better chance of retaining your best people. Studies have shown that job satisfaction and morale improve when people are allowed to stretch and expand their skills. In particular, high performers—the very people you want to keep—become frustrated if they are not allowed to grow and develop.

A second reason for delegating is that when you delegate, your time is freed for more important matters. While you may like the hands-on involvement in the day-to-day details of your business, you can become so involved in the details that you can't see the big picture. A key leadership role you must play if your business is to succeed is that of visualizing the future. You must have time to step back from the daily routine and look ahead—six months, a year, five years. If your business is to grow, someone must plan now for the future. That someone is you.

How to Delegate

Assuming you recognize a need to improve your delegation, how do you go about it? Here is a step-by-step process to ensure that you delegate the right things to the right people in the right way.

Step One: Decide What You Can Delegate

In Chapter 16, we provided suggestions for developing your time budget—an inventory of recurring demands on your time. This inventory is a natural starting point for finding tasks you can delegate. Review this list and divide it into two categories—those things you must do (because they are so sensitive and confidential) and everything else. The latter—everything else—are prime candidates for tasks to delegate.

Step Two: Decide Upon the "Results" You Want

No one can successfully perform a task for you unless he or she knows the results you expect. How will they (and you) know when the job is done and done right? Before you can successfully delegate a task, you must be able to communicate your expectations. What are these expectations? Obviously they depend upon the task, but usually they include some or all of the following:

- How much (quantity expectations)
- How well (quality expectations)
- By when (timeliness expectations)
- At what cost (financial expectations)

Step Three: Delegate to the Right Person

In an earlier chapter, we noted that a person's success in performing any job is a function of three "success factors." They were

- The "how to" factor (knowledge and skill)
- The "want to" factor (internal motivation)
- The "able to" factor (natural ability)

We suggested you use these factors in making any hiring decision. You should use the same success factors when you are trying to decide who should be delegated a given task.

An obvious choice of someone to be delegated a task is someone who has the knowledge and skill because they have performed the task well in the past for your company or another company. Chances are, however, you won't have that experience to tap. Therefore, you must focus on the other two success factors. To do so, first ask yourself if any special abilities are required to perform the task. For example, will the person need a facility with numbers or unique verbal ability? Narrow your list to a few top candidates who you feel possess the basic natural ability required. Then ask yourself, "Which of these candidates would most like to perform the task because they obviously enjoy this type of work or they would see performing the task as a way to develop their skills and/or advance?" In short, you should use what you know about the people who report to you to select someone who would really see performing the task as an opportunity.

Once you have made your choice, discuss the task with them and *ask* them if they would be interested in performing it. Don't tell them they have to do it. If for any reason they appear reluctant to take on the task, reconsider your choice. Remember, people are most successful and work harder at doing those things they want to do and have volunteered to do. You are looking for a volunteer who really wants the accountability and responsibility for the task. You are not looking for someone who sees performing the task as just another "burden" to be suffered.

Step Four: Communicate the Results You Expect

The cause of most unsuccessful delegation is usually miscommunication about expected results. Don't let that happen. When you are talking to someone about accepting responsibility for a task, make sure you are very clear about the end results you expect.

If, for example, you are asking them to take on responsibility for preparing a report, show them a previous report prepared the way you want that they can use as a model. Discuss what you liked (and disliked) about reports you have seen in the past.

As you are educating them about your expectations, be sure you cover all of the "result expectations":

- The quantity of work (i.e., the length of the report)
- The quality of the work (i.e., the accuracy of the report and how accuracy is determined)
- The time frame for performing the work (i.e., when the report is due)
- Any cost considerations (i.e., how much can be spent to prepare the report)

Step Five: Discuss and Set Limits of Authority

No one can perform a task without having to make some decisions. But what are the limits of authority they will have to spend money, change the way things are done, handle unusual situations, and so on as they perform the task for you? Usually, in performing any job, there are four levels of authority a person reporting to you might exercise:

1. Authority to take action without informing you (the highest level of authority)
2. Authority to take action and inform you after the fact
3. Authority to decide upon a course of action, inform you, and take action unless you say no
4. Authority to recommend a course of action you must approve

Make sure there is no misunderstanding about the level of authority you are delegating. Discuss with them the authority level you are comfortable with them exercising and they are comfortable with accepting.

Step Six: Agree Upon a Timetable for Follow-up

At least initially, everyone will need some help in performing a new task. You should arrange specific times to follow up on their progress in performing the task at least the first few times they perform it. For example, say: "I think you have a pretty good grasp of the kind of report I need. So why don't you start on pulling the data together and I'll meet with you Wednesday morning to see if you have any further questions."

Some Final Suggestions for Successful Delegation

Here are some further suggestions for making your delegation successful.

Never Delegate at the Last Minute

Whenever you delegate, do so well in advance of when the task must be performed. Whenever anyone takes on a new assignment, it is only natural for them to take longer to accomplish it the first few times they try. You should plan in advance to allow them that little extra time. If you wait until the last minute or delegate in a crisis, you aren't delegating, you are dumping. And when you dump on your employees, you almost guarantee their failure.

Use a Try-out Period

Instead of delegating a whole task at once, try delegating just part of the task, particularly if the job is complex or difficult. By allowing your employee to gradually take on responsibility for performing a job, you minimize your risk—there is less they can do wrong—and you allow them to learn to perform the task in stages rather than all at once.

Never Delegate the Same Task to More Than One Person

When you delegate, don't muddy the waters by splitting accountability and responsibility for performing a task among several people. In particular, never delegate the same task to two or more people at the same time because you want to see who can perform it best. Remember, when everyone is accountable, no one is accountable. Make sure that each of your employees knows exactly what he or she is responsible for doing and that he or she alone will be responsible for getting the job done.

Make Sure Your Other Employees Know When You Have Delegated Responsibility for a Task and Ask for Their Support

When you delegate someone responsibility for performing a job you used to perform, make sure you inform your other employees of your decision. In many cases, the employee who will now be performing the job will need the help and cooperation of others. Make sure he or she gets it. Send out a memo or make an announcement letting other people know that "Mary will now be preparing the monthly financial report." Request that they cooperate with her by providing her with the information and assistance she requires.

Be Lavish with Praise and Stingy with Criticism

Recognize that no one is likely to perform a task exactly right the first time. When you delegate, expect some mistakes. When they happen, resist your temptation to criticize. Instead, emphasize those parts of the job that were done right and help people correct their mistakes. When they do get it right, be lavish with your praise and be sure to "give them the credit."

If you follow these suggestions, you have a good chance of freeing some of your time, developing your employees, and getting a job done correctly and on time. Then when the customers are lined up at the door and the orders are flowing in, you won't have to do it all by yourself. You'll have trained employees ready to share the load.

_18_

Dealing With Difficult People

They come in every shape, form, and size. They can be employees, customers, business associates, or even friends and neighbors. Regardless of who they are, you hate dealing with them. They are the difficult, exasperating, and irritating people. You know them all too well.

What about that one customer you just can't stand to see walk in the door? You know the one. He's the customer who stands in your store screaming at you because you don't happen to stock the part he needs. He's the one who goes on and on about how you give him lousy service when you have already explained five times that (a) there just isn't enough demand for you to carry that kind of part and (b) if he will just drive across town to the specialty part store you recommended, you are sure he can get the part he wants. It would be bad enough if this was the first time this customer had created a scene in the middle of your store, but he is the same one who was in last week yelling about something else.

Then there is Jane, the one employee you've got who gives you the most trouble. It isn't that she is a bad employee. She does her job. But she is a constant complainer. Nothing—literally nothing—is ever right as far as Jane is concerned. She will go on hour after hour about one thing and then another. Nothing will ruin your day as much as getting out of your car and seeing Jane standing at the front door of the office ready to pounce on you as soon as you enter about something else she doesn't like. Okay, maybe some of the things she complains about are really problems that should be corrected. It's just that Jane never seems to want to do anything herself to solve a problem. She just wants to dump one thing after another on you. In fact, you are beginning to think Jane just loves to find things to make your life miserable.

Then there are all the others:

> Ted, the bully who attacks people and throws tantrums.
> Neal, the guy who's always ready to shoot down every idea anyone has with the standard phrase "it won't work."
> Bill, the know-it-all who makes it clear that as far as he is concerned, he's superior to everyone else.

If these "difficult" people are just casual acquaintances, you can suffer your occasional contact with them or better yet, avoid them completely. But what if these people are customers, employees, important suppliers, or others you have to do business with? What do you do then?

In this chapter, we share some suggestions for defusing and coping with all those people who make your life miserable and can get in the way of you accomplishing your business objectives.

Don't Get Angry

Yes, we know it's hard not to get angry when you are dealing with a truly difficult person, particularly if what the person is saying or doing comes across as a personal attack. But you aren't going to be able to resolve the situation if you become emotional. When faced with difficult people, your first objective should be to keep your cool and stay in control of the situation. If you let difficult people make you angry, you will soon find that you have lost control over what is happening. Plus, you will be playing right into their hands. They may want to make you angry. Don't lose control. Play by your rules, not theirs.

Depersonalize

One way not to get angry is to depersonalize the situation. Focus on the facts of the situation, not how they are presented to you.

What happened or didn't happen? When? Where? Who was involved? You aren't going to be able to deal with a difficult person unless you can somehow distance yourself from the encounter so you can view the situation objectively. To help you put that distance between your emotions and the unpleasant encounter, try taking notes as if you were a reporter. Listen, then jot down the *who, what, when, where,* and even the *why* as told to you by the difficult person. Don't evaluate or react—just record. Not only will the act of objectively recording the facts of the situation help you take your mind off the emotion of the encounter, but your notes will provide a basis for your response and eventually for arriving at a solution to the "real" problem.

Remain Quiet and Let Them Blow off Steam

Sometimes, the best thing you can say in encounters with difficult people is nothing at all. Give them time to wind down. Don't agree or disagree. Just look at them and listen. Very few people can sustain a one-sided argument for long. If they are angry, they will eventually need fuel for their anger. Don't give it to them. Don't launch in with a "Now, wait a minute . . ." or "I'm not going to stand here and listen to that . . ." or "We certainly didn't do that . . ." If you do, you may only provide them with the opportunity to launch into another tirade. Just listen. Take a few notes, as we suggested previously. Don't ignore them. If they think you are ignoring them, your inattention may just further fuel their anger. Just look at them, show you are paying attention, and give them time. Most difficult people will soon run out of steam. Besides, they'll begin to realize that they are starting to look a little foolish. If they don't seem to be running down, wait until there is a pause in their conversation—they have to take a breath sooner or later, don't they?—then jump in to paraphrase what they have said. Don't disagree or try to make your point. Just say, "Now, let me review what you have said. As I understand it, you feel that . . ."

If You Are Wrong, Admit It

None of us like to admit that we were wrong. Maybe that is why we are so disarmed when someone actually admits to us that they made a mistake, did something wrong, or failed to do something they should have done. If in the course of the difficult person's outburst—as you sit or stand there recording the facts—you suddenly realize they're right about a point or two, wait until they calm down, then admit your error, apologize, and state what you are prepared to do to correct the error. Say, "You're perfectly right. I didn't . . . I'm sorry. Suppose I . . . would that help to set things right?" You'll be surprised at their reaction and, perhaps, their begrudging admiration. Plus, when you are wrong and admit it, you put an end to at least that part of the argument.

Empathize

Even if you are not wrong, try to empathize with their feelings. Try to put yourself in their shoes. Perhaps relate what they must be feeling to how you have felt. Often, people who are angry, upset, or chronically complaining about one thing or another feel frustrated and that they lack control over the situation. Let them know you understand how they are probably feeling. Say something like, "I understand how frustrating it is when . . . I've experienced similar situations myself and I know how I felt." Of course, you have to be honest about the situation. Have you really encountered a similar problem? How did you really feel? Don't make up a situation and don't launch into a lengthy discussion of your problems or what happened to you. Your purpose in expressing sympathy is only to establish some common ground of feeling so that you can move on to problem-solving.

Be Assertive

In dealing with difficult people, you don't have to just take it. You have a right to express your point of view, and you should do so. First, listen to what they have to say. Let them "run down." Admit mistakes you may have made and offer to correct them. Empathize with their feelings. Then state how you feel or think. However, don't argue with what they said or criticize them. Just state your views clearly and firmly. For example, say, "I know you think we should . . . , but I disagree." You aren't challenging them or belittling their opinion. You are just stating your opinion. If you do happen to agree with them on certain points, say so. Say, "I agree that we . . . , however, I don't agree that . . ." Make your statements short, simple, and to the point. Asserting yourself and making your opinions clear are particularly important if you are dealing with a bully or know-it-all. With them, any hesitation on your part will be seen by them as a weakness to be exploited. With a bully or know-it-all, you have to be firm.

Get Them to Focus on Solving the Problem

Eventually, you need to get to problem-solving. If your difficult person is a chronic complainer, you want to get beyond the complaints to some type of action. If you are dealing with an irate customer, you want to calm the situation and move to a resolution that will work for you and the customer. As you move to problem-solving, be sure to involve the difficult people in the process. First, get their agreement on the real problem. Say, "As I understand it, we have agreed that the problem is . . . do you agree?" Once you have reached agreement on the problem, ask them for a suggested resolution. Say, "What do you think should be done?" All too often, difficult people—particularly chronic complainers—will try to dump their problems on you. Don't let them. Get them to participate in finding a resolution. If you don't agree with a solution they propose, present an alternative. Say, "I wouldn't be comfortable with doing that. But what if we . . . how would you feel about that?" If they propose a solution and you can agree in part, say so. Try to build upon common ground by pointing out where there is agreement about a desired end result or steps toward a solution. Then seek to resolve those points where you are still in disagreement. If you can't reach an immediate solution, try at least to continually narrow the gap until remaining areas of disagreement are trivial. Say, "We agree that what needs to happen is . . . we also agree that . . . where I see us disagreeing is . . . how do you think we can resolve that?"

A Note of Caution

Rarely do difficult people become violent. They may be exasperating and irritating, but rarely will they do anyone physical harm. Yet it is possible for a disagreement, argument, or confrontation to suddenly accelerate out of control. And unfortunately, stresses people face day-to-day may cause them to act irrationally occasionally. Since there is always the remote possibility that a difficult situation may become a dangerous situation, it is doubly important for you to stay in control. If, for any reason, you are uncomfortable dealing with a difficult person alone or behind closed doors, don't do it. Have someone you trust join you or, if you must, deal with the difficult person within sight of a public area. If you start to deal with a situation and you feel you are losing control or you are uncomfortable with the situation for any reason, end the discussion. Walk away. Just say, "I think we should continue this at a later time," or "I don't think this is the time for either of us to discuss this." Then leave. Just be sure you stay in control and stop anything before it gets out of hand.

__19__

Super Service:
It's Just Good Theater

Customers can be demanding, irritating, exasperating, and at times a total nuisance. They are also the lifeblood of your business. Here are a few facts about the importance of customer satisfaction to your business:

1. Customers are more likely to quit doing business with your company because of poor service than for any other reason.
2. Your customers will be willing to pay as much as a 10 percent price premium for "outstanding service."
3. Customers who are ecstatic about the service you provide are your company's best investment in advertising. On the average, each one of your satisfied customers will recruit five additional customers for your business.
4. Your customers' perceptions of your business are shaped more by the service you provide than by the quality or cost of your company's products or services.

Providing superior customer service is critical to the success of any business, particularly today when there is so much competition and your customers have so many options concerning where and with whom they spend their time and money. How, then, do you ensure that your company provides superior customer service? It's simple. Just think of great customer service as great theater.

It All Starts with a Good Script

Great theater starts with a good script. The same is true of great service. In the case of customer service, your script is your written service plan. It spells out the details of the experience your customers will have in doing business with your company, just as a script spells out in detail what the audience will experience. Ask yourself what your customers' experience should be like. What should happen first, second, and third? Who are the players and what are their parts? Write your service plan the way you might write a script for a play, by thinking of the whole process of the customer's interaction with your business as a series of scenes. Better yet, storyboard the whole process from the point at which the customer enters your store or first contacts your business until the final sale and the "happy" customer departs.

Your customer service plan should be very much like a good script, with all the elements necessary to provide your customers (audience) with an enjoyable experience—one they would want to repeat time and again. In order to make that experience enjoyable, you have to understand the customers' wants and needs. Is it a calm and relaxed atmosphere? Is it a slow or a fast pace? Is it a lot of personal attention or quick and convenient self-service? The more you listen to your customers and the more you learn about their desires, needs, and wants, the better your "script" for superior customer service will be.

Your whole objective in developing your customer service script should be to provide your customers with an experience that *exceeds* their expectations. And remember that your customers do have certain expectations, just as patrons of the theater have expectations. A comedy should be funny. A drama should touch the audience's emotions. An adventure must have action. A mystery must have suspense. When a customer contacts or visits your business, he or she has certain preconceived expectations about the nature of the interaction he or she will experience or should experience. Those expectations are developed from contacts he or she has had with businesses similar to yours. Think about banks, convenience stores, auto repair shops, Mexican restaurants. You probably have a clear image of what each of these should look like and what you will experience by visiting them. Some of those expectations are favorable; some are unfavorable. In writing your script, you want to meet or *exceed* the favorable expectations your target customers have for your type of business while avoiding the unfavorable experiences your customers have had with your competitors. If you get to know your customers very well, you will be able to see business transactions through their eyes. Then you will be able to script the transaction with your business to make the experience of doing business with your company one your customers will never forget.

Cast the Parts

The script you write for customer service is only words without stage actors to speak the words and play the parts. Your employees are your "actors." It is a good idea to encourage your employees to think of their job of servicing customers as one of playing a part. Actors have good days and bad days, but the show must go on. The same is true of servicing customers. When you go to the theater, you don't want to know that the lead actor doesn't feel well, or just had a fight with his spouse, or is upset because the leading lady upstaged him during the last performance. All you want to do is sit back and enjoy the show. You want the actors to do what you are paying for them to do—entertain you. Customers have the same expectations. Tell your employees what the Disney people tell their employees: "When you are in contact with the customers, you are on stage. Your job is to play your part the way it is written. Everything else is to be handled 'backstage'— at home, in the employee lounge, in the manager's office, etc. We want nothing to interfere with the customers' experience."

As you might expect, servicing customers is demanding. Since it is—and since it is so important to the success of your business— picking the right people to service your customers is critical. First, not every employee is qualified by training, experience, or personality to service customers. Some people should never go on stage. Use them backstage. Second, match your employees to the parts they must play. Every employee is not right for every role.

You may have sales roles, technical support roles, installer roles, training roles, after-sale support roles. To the extent possible, you should match your personnel to the roles they are most qualified to play. And remember, your customer has expectations about how your employees will behave in each of these roles. You want your employees to meet and, if possible, exceed your customers' expectations.

Rehearsal

Regardless of how well you are able to match your employees to the roles they are to play, they can't be successful without a lot of rehearsal. Training is critical and, particularly in small businesses, is often neglected. In our rush to just place a body in front of our customers, too often we place new and untrained workers "on the floor" right away with disastrous results. A common complaint of employees we interview is that they received little or no training before being placed in a critical customer service role. Somehow we expect these new employees to just tough it out. In the end, customers suffer. And when customers suffer, our business suffers. Imagine a director allowing actors to just show up opening night, be handed a copy of the script, and march on stage to perform without a single hour of rehearsal time. We could hardly expect a flawless performance even from the most skilled actor. In short, if you want to provide good service to customers, you have to train your employees well and give them plenty of time to rehearse.

When employees rehearse, they shouldn't do so in front of the audience. Imagine going to the theater and hearing the following before the opening curtain: "Tonight the role of Johnny will be played by Mr. Bill Smith. Mr. Smith is new to our company and hasn't had a chance to rehearse his part. Therefore, we hope you will excuse him if he forgets some of his lines. To help Mr. Smith until he has had an opportunity to learn his part, the Assistant Director, Ms. Joan Lewis, will stand next to him on the stage, whisper the dialogue to him, and tell him what to do. We hope this temporary situation will not interfere with your enjoyment of the play and that you will treat Mr. Smith with sympathy and understanding as he learns his part." Sound absurd? We might have sympathy for poor Mr. Smith, but feel contempt for his director. Yet in business, too often we place a new, untrained employee on the checkout counter or on the floor to wait on customers with, perhaps, another worker or assistant manager to whisper instructions in his ear and prompt him on every move. We ask the customer to have patience and understanding as we "rehearse" our new employee on the customer's time. That's just bad service. We should train employees "backstage" or before the show begins.

Also, every actor who is on stage should be ready to work—ready to play his or her part. No director would allow actors who weren't needed in a scene to wander around the stage drinking coffee, chatting with other actors, or talking on the telephone while the play is in progress. Yet in business, we allow workers to eat, smoke, drink coffee, talk to their friends, make personal telephone calls, and do any number of things right "on stage" in front of the customer. Such employee indifference sends a clear message to our customers that they are unimportant. In order to provide great customer service, you should make sure that every employee a customer can see is ready, willing, and able to respond to the customers' needs whatever they may be. Employees should never be allowed to take a break "on stage" in front of customers. Work that is not related to serving the customer should be performed "off stage" or after hours. If that's not possible, then the employee performing such work should be required to respond to the customer first. Any employee a customer can see should have one top priority—"Make the customer's experience in doing business with us enjoyable."

Set the Stage

A good script, casting, and lots of rehearsal are just the beginning of making a good play. To make the play work, we have to have the right wardrobe, sets, and props. Not only must we have these things, but they must be chosen with the greatest of care. The best wardrobe, set, and props not only add to the play—help tell the story—but they also should form an endless seam with the actors and dialogue to help create the experience for the audience. They should not stand out from or conflict with the mood we are trying to create. When they do, they can destroy the experience for the audience no matter how great the script or actors. For example, a friend of ours once attended a version of *Hamlet* offered by a famous Shakespearean company. The dialogue was traditional—just as Shakespeare wrote it. But the set, the actors' wardrobe, and the props used on the stage were decidedly modern. The effect, to say the least, was jarring for our friend (an admitted traditionalist) and greatly undermined his enjoyment of the performance.

In business, the sets, wardrobe, and props are the work environment, uniforms, and equipment we provide our employees. Not only must these be good, reliable, and easy for our employees to use, but most importantly, they must be selected and designed from the viewpoint of the customer. All too often, a great plan for customer service is undermined by inattention to how the methods, processes, procedures, and technology we use to service customers interferes with their experience in doing business with us. Too often, we design business systems to meet the company's needs or employees' needs without ever thinking about how they impact customer needs. If you want to provide great customer service, make sure you test everything that is done against the customers' criteria. Ask yourself: "What would the customer think of that? How would that affect the customers' enjoyment of the business transaction?"

Have a Full Dress Rehearsal or Out-of-Town Tryout Before Your Major Opening Night

No playwright would want his play presented for the first time on Broadway. Regardless of how good the playwright, director, and actors might be, there is always an advantage in having a tryout or dress rehearsal before the big opening night. The same should be true of business practices. Before you make a change in a business practice or introduce a new system or technology, test it. Then test it a second, third, and fourth time. And test it under the worst possible conditions. Then at night or on a holiday when the business is closed, hold a formal dress rehearsal with some employees playing the part of customers and doing the dumbest, most complicated things they can think of. Try to make the new system or method fail from the customer's viewpoint. Then fix any errors before you use the new system. If you have several business locations, try out the new methods or systems in your least vulnerable location first. We'll leave it to you to decide what makes a location "least vulnerable." Just make sure that if something goes wrong—and it will—the failure will do the least damage to your business and offend the fewest customers. If your business is cyclical, don't install a new method, technology, or procedure during the most critical time of the month or year. Remember, when you make a change, you want the customer to notice only the improved service, not the change itself.

Listen to Your Critics

No one particularly likes critics. But they can't and shouldn't be ignored. In the theater, actors, directors, writers, and producers, all are anxious to read the early reviews. They want to know what the critics have to say. In your business, you also should want to know what your critics have to say. It's smart to invite critics in to look at what you are doing and give you advice. Thus, periodically as you can afford it, have an outside industry consultant look at what you are doing and offer you some advice. If you can't afford to hire a consultant, see if someone from the small business development center in your area will take a look at the service component of your business and give you some advice for free or at a reduced rate. If that's not possible, see if you can trade with a business associate—he or she agrees to shop your business and give you feedback and you agree to do the same for his or hers. The point is to periodically find someone you trust who can give you some impartial advice about what you might be doing right or wrong. Of course, even the smartest critic isn't always right. There have been many good plays critics hated that have gone on to become roaring successes. But you will always benefit from an outsider's view. You may not agree with what he or she had to say, but at least his or her criticism will challenge your assumptions and make you justify your actions.

When you are criticized and realize you are wrong, admit it and change what you are doing. Don't be like the playwright who so loved his second act that he was unwilling to delete a single line of dialogue even when the producers said the play was much too long. Because of his stubborn refusal to change a word, his play stayed just as he had written it—on paper sitting on a shelf and unproduced. Sure, it hurts to abandon something you have worked hard to develop, but sometimes that is the price you must pay to get superior customer service.

Enjoy the Applause

The payoff for a great play is a standing ovation and a long run on Broadway. Well, in business you may not be able to get your customers to applaud you each time you walk by. But if you treat your customers like an opening night audience and you approach serving them as if you were providing great entertainment, your business might just have a long and profitable run. And isn't that what you're really after?

__20__

After the Flack . . . Win Them Back

Regardless of how well you run your company, sooner or later you or one of your employees will make a customer unhappy. How you respond when that customer complains may mean the difference between the success and failure of your business in the long term.

Ignore a customer's complaint and you will not only lose that customer but ten or twenty others as well. Also, potential customers will probably hear about your company's reputation for poor service. Many of them will never do business with your company again.

When you resolve a customer's complaint to his or her satisfaction, however, you have a good chance of retaining that customer. When their complaints are quickly and satisfactorily resolved, 95 percent of your unhappy customers will do business with you again. Plus, they will tell their friends that your company can be counted on to do the right thing. Here are some suggestions for ensuring that your company resolves complaints quickly.

Develop a Complaint Policy

When a customer complains about poor service or a defective product in person or by phone, you have only a few seconds to respond. If the complaint is by letter, you have a few days at most. You can't wait until you receive a complaint to decide how you are going to respond; instead, you should have a complaint policy in place, and all of your employees should know immediately how to respond when they receive a complaint.

What should your policy be? Simple. In today's competitive environment, you should be prepared to do whatever is necessary and reasonable to resolve the complaint to the customer's satisfaction.

Isn't such a policy extreme? Yes and no. Yes, in the sense that by adopting such a policy, you are setting your company up to be cheated occasionally. Your "customers first" policy will probably mean that you'll make it easy for customers to return items, no questions asked. Some of your customers will take unfair advantage of your return policy and return items they didn't buy from you, or items that have been used. Being cheated once in a while is the price of building a reputation for service.

But take heart. Placing the customer's needs first isn't an extreme policy, when you consider that only a few customers will take unfair advantage of you. Research suggests that less than 5 percent of customers who return items try to take advantage of a company by returning items they bought elsewhere or have already used. The remaining 95 percent have a legitimate problem with an item they bought in the store. The goodwill you establish with these honest customers by making it easy for them to get their problems resolved will more than make up for the few dishonest customers who will try to cheat you. Besides, you know how hard—and how expensive—it is to get a customer. Can you afford to lose even one?

In establishing your policy for handling customer complaints, you should go beyond merely adopting a slogan. It's okay to preach to your employees that "the customer is always right," but what does that really mean? What are you prepared to do to resolve a customer's problem? More important, what are you empowering your employees to do? What steps can they take to correct a problem without consulting you?

At Holiday Inn the hotel staff is empowered to take a range of actions to satisfy an unhappy customer. These actions are specified in advance. For example, the staff might start by offering a certificate for a free drink or free meal to a customer who had a problem. If that doesn't satisfy the customer, they can reduce or eliminate a charge for a service. In serious cases, the hotel manager can waive the entire charge for the night's lodging.

To form an effective policy for handling customer complaints, you must think through the types of problems that might occur and decide on possible remedies. Then authorize your employees to take action without seeking your permission.

Follow the "Recipe for Recovery"

Ron Zemke, author of *The Service Edge,* suggests using the following five-step "Recipe for Recovery" when customers complain:

1. *Apologize.* When a customer complains, the first thing you and your staff should say is "I'm sorry." This is a simple statement, but it sends a powerful message to the customer. Among other things, it says "We care." Yet how often do you remember to apologize when faced with a customer's complaint? More likely, you immediately set about solving the problem, with a scowl on your face that sends the message "Here we go again—another crazy customer."

   Perhaps you start investigating the problem. The customer returns an item, saying it doesn't work. You say, "Let me take a look at that. You say it doesn't work? That's strange. We sell hundreds of these and nobody else has had a problem." In effect, you are telling the customer, "You idiot. You probably couldn't work one of these things if your life depended on it." Or worst of all, you may just quote company policy, in your most authoritative "schoolteacher" voice.

   If you don't say those two simple words, "I'm sorry," you lose the opportunity to turn a complaint into a positive experience for the customer. Obviously, "I'm sorry" doesn't solve the customer's problem. But a sincere personal apology can help diffuse the customer's anger and put you on the road to a positive solution.

2. *Listen to the customer and empathize with his or her problem.* A sincere apology sends the message that you care. Empathy

sends the message that you can put yourself in the customer's place and understand how he feels. Empathy is important because you must first deal with the customer's feelings before you can address the problem objectively.

3. *Make an effort to resolve the problem.* Zemke calls this step "Urgent Reinstatement." Urgency is the key here. You must show the customer that you intend to take steps to correct the problem immediately. You may not succeed, but you will "try hard" and "do the best you can," sending the customer away with the knowledge that you did all you could.

An apology, empathy, and a valiant effort to solve a problem will often be enough to satisfy an unhappy customer, particularly if the problem caused no more than a minor inconvenience or irritation for the customer. However, if the problem was truly serious—if the customer felt not just annoyed, but victimized—then you may have to go further. For these serious problems, Zemke recommends taking two final steps.

4. *Make symbolic atonement.* This gesture tells the customer, "We want to make it up to you." A coupon, a free drink, an offer to waive part of a bill—all of these symbolic gestures can help smooth over ill feelings and restore relationships.

5. *Follow up.* In the case of a serious problem, a follow-up call to the customer is a good way to smooth over the whole incident. The follow-up call provides another opportunity to tell the customer, "We care about you," and "We are sorry a problem occurred." More important, it provides an opportunity for the employee involved in the confrontation with the unhappy customer to bring the incident to a conclusion. Few employees intentionally create problems for customers, and most employees are embarrassed if they create a problem due to an oversight or inattention.

Make a Real Commitment

Ron Zemke's five steps to recovery represent a good approach to managing encounters with unhappy customers. But Zemke's approach is only a technique. As good as the technique might be, if you truly want to turn unhappy customers into loyal customers, then you and your employees must be committed to satisfying customers, regardless of how much it costs in time, effort, and money.

_21_

True Quality

In a preceding chapter, we said your customers would pay more for outstanding service—possibly as much as 10 percent more. They will also pay more—in some cases substantially more—for outstanding quality. How much more will they pay for great quality? In a 1988 survey, the average American said he or she would pay as much as 20 percent more for a better car, 40 percent more for a better dishwasher, and 66 percent more for a better pair of shoes. The fact is, today Americans want both great service and great quality. They'll settle for one or the other—maybe. But what they really want is both. Think of what it would mean to your business if you could give your customers exactly what they want— great service and great quality. They would be so happy, they would just keep coming back for more. And they might just be willing to pay extra for the privilege. Imagine having a whole store (or shop or office) full of loyal, happy customers just waiting to pay a little extra to do business with you. And all that extra would just go to your bottom line. If you have started "entertaining" your customers with great service, you are already on you way to building this winning service/quality combination. We will show you how to offer your customers the second half of that combination—world-class quality.

Service versus Quality

Before we begin, perhaps we should clarify the distinction between service and quality. They are really two separate parts of the customer's expectations in dealing with your business. And they apply whether your business is in manufacturing or the service sector. If you manufacture a product, you are or should be providing your customer with product service and product quality. If you provide a service, there is or should be both a service and quality component to what you provide. Sound confusing? Not really. Think of it this way. When a customer does business with you, he or she has at least two major expectations. First, he or she expects (or at least hopes) that the experience of doing business with you will be a pleasant and enjoyable one. That's the expectation for service. Second, the customer expects value from the transaction. That's the expectation for quality. Your business can meet one, both, or neither of these expectations. If your customer enjoys the transaction—feels you and your employees were cooperative, helpful, pleasant, nice, friendly—then chances are the customer will feel he or she got great service. If your customer feels he or she got real value for the money—the product performed as he or she expected or the service met his or her need—then the customer is likely to think that he or she got great quality.

What Is Great Quality?

The true definition of quality is in the customers' eyes. The customer and only the customer defines quality. It doesn't make any difference what you or your employees think. Thus, you are providing good-quality products or services only if you are meeting or exceeding your customers' expectations. The key question then is, "What are your customers' expectations?"

Defining your customers' expectations is a difficult and time-consuming process. And it is a process you have to keep performing over and over. One problem with defining customer expectations is that there are so many of them. Your customer doesn't use just one criteria to decide if you provide quality products and services. He or she uses multiple criteria. Some of these criteria are logical;

some totally emotional. Think about the criteria you use in eval-
uating the quality of an automobile you are considering purchasing.
You aren't just looking at the car's frequency-of-repair record.
You are probably also interested in the car's construction, style,
ease of operation, and appropriateness for your transportation
needs. But you don't stop there, do you? Admit it. Isn't purchasing
a car also an emotional decision? In addition to its reliability,
styling, and all those other things, you are also concerned about
how the car makes you feel. As the commercial says, "It just has
to feel right." Plus, you probably are concerned about how it makes
others feel—your spouse, your friends, and so on. There are multiple facets to your evaluation of the quality of a car you're considering purchasing. The same is true for other products and
services you purchase. And the same is true for your customers.
They also have multiple needs and expectations concerning the
"quality" of the products and services they buy from you.

A second problem with getting to know your customers' expectations is that they are constantly changing. Your customers' needs
change over time, and with the change in their needs their expectations change. Also, your customers become smarter consumers
the more they do business with you. Never forget that in the process
of doing business with a customer, you are simultaneously educating that customer about your business and about what he or
she can expect from your business. For example, we have frequently encountered clients who casually began to offer additional
free services to their customers only to regret later that they hadn't
given more thought to how those free services would change their
customers' expectations. Of course, there is nothing wrong with
providing additional free services as a carefully orchestrated strategy to get a leg up on the competition. The problem for some of
our clients is that the "free" services just happened. Sales or service
representatives just decided on their own to start doing something
for the customer free of charge they had never done before and
that, perhaps, the customer had never even asked for them to do.
Suddenly, the "free" service became a customer expectation. The
company couldn't stop offering the service or even start charging
for it without risking offending the customer. Of course, you may
be locked in to providing a free or additional service to your customers because your key competitors are. That's another way cus-

tomer expectations change. Chances are, your customers are not doing business solely with you. They are also doing at least some business with your competitors and they are learning new expectations from them.

If you are to understand your customers' expectations, you have to get to know your customers very well. You have to meet your customers personally. You have to ask them what they think about the quality of the products and services you are providing. And whenever possible, you need to observe them actually using your product or service. Don't depend upon your sales force, service personnel, or customer relations people to tell you what customers think. Find out yourself and make sure all of your key decision makers spend a large portion of their time talking to and getting to know customers directly. Excellent quality can't be built unless the top people in your organization—you included—have a close personal relationship with your customers and clear, unfiltered access to knowledge about what the customer wants. When you are planning a new product or service, it is absolutely critical that you bring customers into the design and development process. Ask them what they think of the proposed new product or service. Let them play with product prototypes. Find out what they are thinking and feeling, then design your product or service accordingly.

Planning for World-Class Quality

Excellent quality doesn't happen by accident. You have to plan for it. Quality as defined by your customers' needs should be the primary tool you use for planning. At least once a year you should review and revise a two- to five-year written plan for your business. Part of that plan should be a product-by-product, service-by-service review of what your company offers its customers. Get away from your business for two to three days every year—we know that's hard to do, but you must do it. Take your top people with you. Also, take all of the data and information you have about your customers and their needs. Then sit down with your decision makers and review everything your company is doing. Look at the products and services your company is currently providing and those proposed for the future. Test each product and service against your customers' expectations as you understand them. Ask yourself if each product or service you are now providing is meeting the needs it was designed to meet. Have the customers' needs changed? If so, how? Has the product or service been changed in line with the customers' changing expectations? What about the new products or services? What needs or expectations of customers will they meet? Once you have reviewed all of your products and services, both old and new, then start developing your plan. You should come out of your two- to three-day session with an action plan (activity, responsibility, target date for completing) that spells out how you will eliminate those products or services that no longer meet your customers' expectations and rapidly develop those new products or services your customers need.

Quality Leadership

Quality, as we said, can only be defined as "meeting or exceeding customer expectations." It is as much an attitude, concept, or philosophy as it is a set of management principles or practices. It doesn't happen without top-level commitment. If you want a genuine concern for meeting customer expectations (true quality) to permeate your company, that concern has to start with you. You have to exhibit in what you say, do, and reward people for saying and doing, that you are obsessed with quality. Nothing less than your total commitment in words and actions will do. Let down just once—belittle a customer, knowingly ship a product that isn't quite right, place sales or profits above quality—do any of these things just once and you will send a message that quality doesn't really matter.

Perhaps the most important thing you can do to send a message to your employees that quality does matter is to measure quality and base the rewards and recognition you provide employees on performance on these quality measures. You should have at least two types of measures—external and internal. External quality measures are those that indicate customer satisfaction with the quality of the products/services you are providing. Examples of external measures include problem reports from customers, customer returns, customer ratings, and warranty costs. Internal quality measures are indicators of quality before the product or service reaches the customer. Examples of internal measures are rework, waste, scrap, and something we call the cost of nonconformance.

The cost of nonconformance is the difference between the actual cost you incur in producing and selling a product or service and the cost if everything was done right the first time. Your actual cost is the cost of labor, materials, supplies, equipment, and everything else that goes into manufacturing the product or providing the service. To the extent possible, you should structure your accounting system and cost reporting so that you can tie costs directly to individual lines of products or services without allocating indirect or overhead costs. The reason for this is that if you allocate large blocks of costs across your products and services, you may never have a true indicator of what a specific type of product or service is costing. (For a good summary of the issues involved in accounting for costs, call the American Productivity & Quality Center in Houston, Texas at (713) 681-4020 and ask for a copy of BRIEF 67, "Productivity's New Math," by John Miller, October 1988.)

Once you have established your actual cost for producing a product or service, your next step in calculating the cost of nonconformance is to determine what is called your "no-failure cost." Your no-failure cost has three parts: (1) appraisal costs—the cost of inspection and testing you perform on purchased items or products you produce to catch bad quality before it can reach the customer; (2) failure cost—the cost to your company of any bad quality that does reach the customer such as the cost of corrective action you have to take plus the cost of bad quality that is caught before it reaches the customer such as scrap and rework; and (3) prevention cost—the cost of everything you do to prevent appraisal or failure costs, such as training you provide your people in quality improvement. For a good explanation of how to calculate the cost of nonconformance, see Chapter 3 of John Groocock's book, *The Chain of Quality*.

Once you have created a good set of quality measures, you should begin giving your people feedback on these measures on a regular basis. We suggest you develop graphs for each of these measures and that you post these graphs in some conspicuous location such as a break area or lunchroom. You should also set goals for performance on each of these measures and show the goal or target on the graphs you develop. You should then use these graphs to review performance on your quality measures in regular weekly or monthly meetings you conduct with your employees.

Involving Employees in Continuous Improvement Efforts

Real improvement in the quality measures you develop won't come about overnight. Quality improvement is a gradual and never-ending process. As we have suggested previously, no company ever reaches the point where further improvement in quality isn't needed or required. You need a lot of ideas and suggestions to find ways to improve continuously. That's where your employees come in. Weekly or monthly, as you meet with your employees and share information about the quality of your products and services, you need to engage them in problem-solving efforts to find ways to improve. Don't be surprised if your employees are poor problem solvers at first. Most of us are. The sad fact is that very few Americans ever learn problem-solving skills. Consequently, at first all you may be able to hope for is to get your employees suggesting ideas for improving quality. Eventually, you will want to become more sophisticated in your problem-solving efforts. For that, you and your employees will probably require some training. Watch for public seminars in your area you can attend or have at least some of your employees attend that focus on quality-improvement techniques or problem-solving skills. If you need specific suggestions on the type of training you should try to provide your employees, obtain a copy of Ted Cocheu's article, "Training for Quality Improvement," in the January 1989 issue of the *Training & Development Journal,* which should be available through your local library.

22

Your Business Health Checkup

If you have reached our ages, you probably recognize that it's wise to go in to your doctor for a periodic checkup. You probably realize you need to get a checkup occasionally even if you don't have any symptoms of something wrong. After all, it's better to be safe. If there is something not quite right, maybe you can get it fixed before it really gets to be a problem. Periodic checkups are a wise health rule. They are also a wise business health rule.

Doing a periodic business health checkup for your own company may be one of the smartest things you can do to insure the survival of your business. And we don't mean just doing a quick check of your finances. Sure, you had better pay attention to sales, revenues, profits, cash flow, and so on. In fact, you had better pay attention to those numbers constantly, not just periodically. Here when we talk about a business health checkup we are talking about checking out how your business is run. We suggest some diagnostic checks you should run periodically on your business, how to interpret the results of those tests, and how to start the treatment process if you find your business has a not-so-obvious sickness.

Diagnostic Test 1

Check your employment records and get the name of your newest and lowest-level employee. Visit him or her and introduce yourself if you haven't already met. Make it as friendly and casual as you can but work into your conversation a question about your business's competition. Who are they? What does your business have to do to be successful? Note his or her response. If your employee looks at you as if you are an alien creature just arrived from another planet and mumbles a few unintelligible words, make a mental note that your business has a serious and potentially life-threatening problem. And make a note that the problem isn't with your inarticulate employee. It's with you. You haven't gotten the message across.

Diagnostic Test 2 (Follow-up to Test 1)

You can bypass this test if your employee (or, more precisely you) flunked Test 1.

Let's assume that you check out pretty well on Test 1. Your employee was able to cite three of your five major competitors and did manage to mumble a few words about how "quality" and "serving customers" were important. That's not too bad. (You would be surprised how many employees wouldn't get that far.) Having passed Test 1 with at least a C, you can now move on to a little more detail. Ask this employee what he or she does or can do to make "quality" or "customer service" (or whatever else your business strategy requires) happen. If he or she launches into a full description of the "quality" and "service" components of his or her job—how "quality" for example will be good if he or she does this or that and not this or that—then congratulate yourself and make a note to congratulate the employee's supervisor on a job well done. However, if the employee who did so well (or reasonably well) on the general response mumbles or launches into a confused muddle in response to the specific question, then you've got a problem. General knowledge isn't any use to your employee (or your business) if it can't be translated into specifics. Being healthy means getting the little things right. And your people have to know what the little things are before they can get them right.

Diagnostic Test 3

This test involves talking to another employee. Since you have probably half scared your newest and lowest-level employee to death with your crazy questions in Diagnostic Tests 1 and 2, we suggest you pick another employee this time. Try picking an employee who has been with you for a while. Go up to him where he works and say, "Well, Joe, how did things go yesterday?" If Joe responds, "Ok, I guess," or "About as usual," or with some general remark such as those, mark down that your business has a sickness you need to cure. If, on the other hand, good old Joe starts quoting you statistics on percentage of Good Quality or On Time Shipment or Daily Production, then enjoy it. You have another one for the health column.

Diagnostic Test 4

This is an easy one. All you have to do is walk through your plant, office, or store. Do your walk-through at night after your business is closed and everyone has gone home. If you can, arrange to do your walk-through after a particularly busy day. What do you see? Is your place of business clean, neat, and orderly? Does it look as if a hurricane just hit? If your employees' workplace is organized, clean, neat, and well arranged—great! If, instead, it looks like your teenager's bedroom, make a note to yourself that you have a problem—and it's not just with your teenager this time, it's with your business. Neatness and cleanness may not be enough to insure the success of a business, but they are a good sign of its overall health. When we work with companies, one of the first things we ask for is a tour of the workplace, and one of the things we look for is the condition of the plant, office, or store. Chaos and disorder are not only signs that your business may be run inefficiently (who could find anything in all of this mess?), but, worse, can be a sign that your people no longer care—they don't take pride in what they do. We have rarely seen a successful business where the workplace was filthy and disorganized. However, we have seen many failing businesses where chaos prevailed.

Diagnostic Test 5

One day in the middle of the week, find an unobtrusive spot in your office, store, or plant and watch what your employees do during the day. Try not to make your presence too obvious. For example, find an excuse to be there doing something. Give the appearance of being preoccupied with whatever you are doing. But while you are there watch and listen. Watch your people waiting on customers and talking on the phone. Watch them making your product or providing service. Resist the temptation to jump in and try to correct problems you see (unless of course what you see is dangerous or could have really serious consequences for your company). Try not to be seen or heard. Just watch and listen. When the day is over make some notes to yourself about the good and "not so good" things you saw and heard. Later we will show you how to use these notes.

Diagnostic Test 6

In our previous tests, you have talked to, watched, and listened to your employees. In this test, you turn to your customers. Pick a few of your customers at random and call them on the phone. Even better, go to see them. Ask them about the last time they did business with your company. How were they treated? Did they get the service they deserved? Were they happy with the product or service your people provided? Why or why not? Ask them to level with you about what they liked and didn't like. Tell them you aren't going to punish any of your people based upon what the customer tells you (unless of course something happened that was illegal or really, really atrocious). You just want to get your customers' honest evaluation so that your business can improve. Make some notes of what you are told. Again record the good and the bad.

Diagnostic Test 7

Call your business number during the busiest part of the day. Order a product. Make an inquiry. Log a complaint. See how quickly the call is answered and how your people respond. Are your people courteous, polite, helpful, sincere? Do they sound as if they care? Does a smile come across the telephone lines that makes you feel good about calling? Or are your people abrupt, noncommunicative, uncaring? Make notes on how you felt after the call.

Diagnostic Test 8

Ask a friend (or, if you must, hire someone) to be your "mystery shopper." Ask him or her to shop in your store, order one of your products, or whatever is appropriate. Then ask him or her to brief you on what happened. Who did what, when, where, how. Ask your mystery shopper how he or she liked dealing with your company and your people. Would he or she do business with your company again without being paid to do so? Why or why not? Keep notes on what your mystery shopper tells you.

Diagnostic Test 9

This one applies only if you produce a product.

In the course of shopping your business, your mystery shopper should have purchased one or more of your products. Of course, when he or she did, you paid for the products. Ask your mystery shopper to give you the products he or she bought from your business. In this test, you want to do some comparative analysis. To do so, you need a similar product for comparison. You get that from one of your competitors (just order it or have your mystery shopper order it). Now put your product side by side with their product. Examine them both. Feel them. Use them. Be honest with yourself. Which product is best? In what way? Make notes on all the differences you see.

Diagnostic Test 10

Spend a day working in your plant or store. Wait on customers. Make the product. Provide the service yourself. Pick a day to do this that is traditionally one of your busiest days. When you finish the day, make some notes about what you learned. What was easy, what was difficult? What went smoothly? When did the disaster occur? Why do you think it happened?

Diagnostic Test 11

Pick a product, service, or operation performed in your company—something you don't know very well or haven't performed in a while. Have the employee who normally performs the work walk you through the process. How does the work get done? What is done first, second, third, and so on? Diagram the work if you can. Ask the employee to show you not just the standard or prescribed way of doing things but all the little secrets and shortcuts. Tell him it's OK. You're not trying to catch anybody doing something wrong. You just want to understand how things work in the "real world." Take lots of notes on what you see and hear. Later, review your notes. Is the process you learned about efficient or inefficient? Where could mistakes or errors creep in?

Diagnostic Test 12

Have your secretary or assistant assemble all the reports you received last month and put them on your desk. Have him or her do the same thing for your correspondence. Once you have two piles—one for reports, one for correspondence—start going through the items one by one. Ask yourself: Why did I receive this? What did I do with it? Which numbers from each report did I use? How? When was the last time I used that number to make an important decision? Should someone other than I have received this report or correspondence? Who? If the report or correspondence was internally generated, do I really need it? Why? Justify it. Would it be something I would have my people start producing for me if they weren't already?

Everything on your desk—all the reports and correspondence—costs your company money if they are produced by your people. Think of them as stacks of hundred- (or better, thousand-) dollar bills.

Using Your Test Results

If you complete all of our diagnostic tests, you should have quite a few notes. We hope you have jotted down a lot of good things about your business—your "good health" signs. You probably also have a lot of trouble spots. Some are minor. Some may make you angry. Now, the question is what you do with all of this information. Simple. You hold a meeting with your people. This shouldn't be just any meeting, however. It's a special meeting. It's your "State of the Business" meeting.

In conducting your State of the Business meeting, it's best if you can get your employees together in small groups of no more than ten or twelve people. If you have more employees than that, just hold several meetings, but keep the size down to ten or twelve people each. Also, keep the meeting informal. This is not the State of the Union address you are making. You just want to talk to them personally about how the business is going. Tell them that at the beginning of the meeting. Also tell them you have some general information to share with them about the business's performance plus some more specific information you have gathered from your business health checkup. Emphasize that you want them to ask any questions they may have and that later in the meeting you are going to ask them for some of their ideas about how to make the company run better.

In your meeting with your employees, do the following *in this order*. First, share as much information as you feel you can about the company's performance over the last quarter or year—sales, profits, cash flow, success/failure in launching new products or services, etc. If you are in doubt about whether something is too sensitive to share, share it. Chances are your competitors know anyway. If you haven't shared such information with your employees before, you may have to explain some terms. For example, don't just throw out a term or figure such as "return on assets" and expect your people to understand. Explain what these figures mean.

The second part of your meeting should be devoted to the *good* things from your business health checkup. Tell your people what you saw, what you heard, and what you found out from your mystery shopper and comparison of yours and your competitor's products that you liked. Ideally you should have these listed on a large flip chart pad. As you go over the list, be as specific as you can and don't be afraid to mention specific individuals when you talk about the good things. Say, for example, "John, you remember the day I worked in the store, well I noticed that every time a customer came in the store that day you [describe specifically what John did]." Then say, "John, I thought that was great and if we all could remember to do that, I bet our sales would really climb. Good job, John." When you are comparing your company's product and that of your competition, bring both of them to the meeting with you. Hold up your product next to theirs. Point out specifically the good things you see in your product compared to theirs.

The final part of your meeting should be devoted to the problems you saw in your business health checkup. Again you should have a list written out on a large flip chart pad with plenty of blank pages behind your list so you can add items as they come up in the meeting. In this section, when you are talking about problems in public, never, never mention anyone by name. Talk instead about how "we are doing as a company" and "our need to learn from our mistakes to get better." Go over the problems you saw. Then ask your employees for their help in two ways. First, tell them you want to go around the room and get their suggestions for things to add to the "problem" list. Tell them that if they concur or disagree with something you have listed, you want to know that. Add anything they mention to your list.

When you have finished discussing your problem list, hand each of your employees a 3 × 5 card. Ask them to review the list of problems and select five they feel are in most need of correction right now. Which five do they feel are most important because they impact what the company is trying to accomplish? Collect the cards and end the meeting with a promise to your employees that you will tabulate the results of their problem selection and have a follow-up meeting to pick a few problem areas to work on.

Our diagnostic checkup procedure is a way to insure the long-term health of your business. If you follow this checkup procedure once a year (just like an annual physical), two things will happen. First, you will always have a laundry list of problems to work on. Second, because you have that list, know the problems, and are working with your people constantly to improve, your business will keep getting better and better. With regular annual business checkups you should be able to avoid a catastrophic business illness. Who knows? Your company might just become the healthiest business specimen around.

Select Bibliography

Boyett, Joseph H. and Henry P. Conn. *Maximum Performance Management*. Macomb: Glenbridge Publishing Ltd., 1988.

Conger, Jay. *The Charismatic Leader*. San Francisco: Jossey-Bass, 1988.

Drucker, Peter. *Management*. New York: Harper & Row, 1974.

Gilbert, Thomas F. *Human Competence: Engineering Worthy Performance*. New York: McGraw-Hill, 1978.

Grayson, Jack and Carla O'Dell. *American Business: A Two-Minute Warning*. New York: The Free Press, 1985.

Groocock, John. *The Chain of Quality*. New York: John Wiley & Sons, 1986.

Harmon, Frederick and Gary Jacobs. *The Vital Difference*. New York: AMACOM, 1985.

Mager, Robert and Peter Pipe. *Analyzing Performance Problems*. Belmont: D. S. Lake Publications, 1984.

Tregoe, Benjamin B. and John W. Zimmerman. *Top Management Strategy*. New York: Simon & Schuster, 1980.

Zemke, Ron and Dick Shaaf. *The Service Edge*. New York: New American Library, 1989.